Mastering Knowledge in the Digital Age:

A Young Professional's Guide to PKM

T.D. Errol

Mastering Knowledge in the Digital Age:

A Young Professional's Guide to PKM

By

T.D. Errol

Errol Publishing

For more information, or to book an event, contact:

T.D Errol

Email: errolpublishing@gmail.com

Book design by T.D. Errol
Cover design by T.D. Errol

ISBN Paperback: 9798863438368

Foreword

As I sit on this picturesque fall day in September, I'm taken back to the days before "personal information management" became a buzzword. My system? A filing cabinet stocked with hanging folders, each bearing labels indicating their contents. Beside it, a bookcase brimming with books and magazines. With just a notepad and pen in hand, I'd jot down insights on diverse subjects, notably restaurant management, workouts, and dietary information. Life was indeed different before the advent of home computers.

With my first computer, the world of note-making expanded into a digital realm. Spreadsheets became my new canvas, and storing information electronically reduced physical clutter. But then came gadgets like the Palm Pilot, and suddenly, my notes were with me everywhere. Yet, with every digital innovation, a different kind of clutter emerged: a collection of gadgets gathering dust in closets.

I'm grateful for the eventual stabilization of platforms, streamlining the myriad ways we store cherished information.

In those earlier days, managing information was unpredictable. There were photocopies, handwritten notes, and haphazard filing. But through this journey, I've grasped the significance of Personal Knowledge Management (PKM). More importantly, I've learned that a system, much like a well-tailored suit, should be custom-fit to its user.

Dive into this book, and I hope you derive as much value from its contents as I did while writing it.

Warm Regards, T.D. Errol

Contents

Introduction

The Knowledge Imperative in the Digital Age

The Digital Age, marked by the rise of computers, the internet, and subsequent technologies, has revolutionized the way businesses and individuals operate. With information at our fingertips, the emphasis on knowledge has become paramount for survival and success.

The Evolving Business Landscape

The modern business landscape is not what it used to be. From startups to multinational corporations, the recent years have seen a tectonic shift in business operations, strategies, and philosophies. This shift can be attributed to two main factors:

Rapid Technological Advancements

Rate of Change: Innovations such as artificial intelligence, the internet of things, augmented reality, and blockchain have emerged and evolved at an unprecedented rate. Moore's Law, which states that the number of transistors on a microchip will double approximately every two years, has often been cited to describe this rapid pace of tech evolution.

Industry Disruption: These technologies have disrupted traditional industries. For instance, the rise of e-commerce platforms like Amazon has changed the retail landscape forever. Similarly, companies like Uber and Airbnb have revolutionized transportation and lodging, respectively.

Globalization: The internet has made the world more interconnected than ever. This connectivity allows for businesses to have a global presence and reach audiences that were previously unreachable.

Information Overload

Volume of Data: Every day, 2.5 quintillion bytes of data are created. This staggering figure is a double-edged sword; while it presents opportunities, it also creates challenges for data management and analysis.

Need for Filtering: The vast amount of available information necessitates efficient filtering systems. Search engines, algorithms, and AI-driven tools play a pivotal role in helping us navigate this sea of data.

Risk of Misinformation: With the flood of information comes the risk of misinformation. Verifying the authenticity and accuracy of data has become a critical concern for both individuals and businesses.

The Value of Knowledge

In such a dynamic landscape, simply having information isn't enough. The true power lies in meaningful knowledge derived from that information.

Knowledge as a Competitive Advantage

Informed Strategy: Businesses equipped with accurate and timely knowledge can anticipate market changes, understand customer preferences, and innovate efficiently.

Operational Efficiency: Knowledge about best practices, technological tools, and efficient processes can lead to reduced costs and improved performance.

Brand Value: In an age where consumers are more informed than ever, businesses that position themselves as knowledge leaders often enjoy enhanced brand loyalty and trust.

Knowledge in Decision-Making

Data-Driven Decisions: Knowledge derived from data analytics allows businesses to make decisions based on hard evidence rather than mere intuition. Tools like big data analytics and predictive modeling enable businesses to foresee trends and act proactively.

Risk Management: Accurate knowledge helps in assessing potential risks and formulating mitigation strategies. For example, financial institutions rely heavily on data and knowledge to gauge credit risks.

Innovation: Knowledge about market gaps, consumer needs, and emerging technologies can guide businesses in creating groundbreaking products and services. Apple's success with products like the iPhone and iPad is a testament to the power of knowledge in innovation.

The Digital Age has reshaped the business landscape and underscored the indispensable value of knowledge. Those who harness this power stand to gain immensely, while those who ignore it risk being left behind.

Introduction to Personal Knowledge Management (PKM)

The tapestry of the modern world is interwoven with threads of information, ideas, and insights. Every day, we are inundated with new knowledge, and while the digital age offers endless opportunities, it also presents unique challenges. For young professionals poised on the precipice of this vast digital horizon, mastering the skill of Personal Knowledge Management (PKM) is akin to wielding a compass in an ever-shifting landscape.

Defining PKM

What is PKM?

PKM isn't just about hoarding information. It's about nurturing a symbiotic relationship with knowledge. We take in information, process it, relate it to what we already know, and then, in turn, contribute back to the vast ocean of global wisdom. Through PKM, we make choices about which knowledge we deem important, where we store it, and how we use it to inform our future decisions and actions.

Imagine your mind as a vast library. Without organization, even the most precious of its books could be lost amidst clutter. PKM helps create a systematic approach, enabling you to access the right information at the right time.

Origins and Development

Historically, humans have always sought ways to manage knowledge. From the ancient libraries of Alexandria to the meticulous records of medieval monks, knowledge management has been a cornerstone of human advancement. But as we progressed into the digital era, a more personal touch was needed. With the boom of the internet, PKM emerged as a beacon for individuals navigating the relentless waves of digital information.

The Digital Age and Knowledge Management

How Technology Has Transformed Knowledge Management

If we could travel back a few decades and present the vast expanse of the internet to someone from the past, they'd be awestruck, maybe even overwhelmed. Today's digital platforms are more than just storage systems; they're ecosystems of interconnected knowledge. Platforms like Wikipedia showcase the collaborative nature of human knowledge, while AI-driven tools predict and curate content tailored for individuals.

But this digitization has its shadows. Fake news, misinformation, data breaches, and the sheer overwhelming volume of content can leave even the most tech-savvy individual disoriented. Thus, effective knowledge management isn't just about knowing—it's also about discerning.

PKM as an Essential Skill

In today's dynamic professional landscape, the young professional isn't judged merely by what they know, but by how they apply, adapt, and grow with their knowledge. PKM is the bridge between passive consumption and active application. It's the filter that separates the vital from the trivial. It empowers professionals to anticipate trends, foster innovation, and remain at the forefront of their fields.

Moreover, as remote work and digital collaborations become the norm, your personal knowledge ecosystem can greatly influence your professional relationships and opportunities. It can shape your personal brand, giving you a distinct edge in a competitive marketplace.

By the end of this exploration into PKM, you won't just understand its importance—you'll be equipped to reshape your relationship with knowledge. As you dive into the subsequent chapters of "Mastering Knowledge in the Digital Age," envision yourself not just as a consumer of information, but as an architect of your own unique knowledge universe. A universe that evolves, adapts, and thrives in tandem with you. Let the journey of shaping your intellectual legacy begin.

Why PKM Matters for Young Professionals

In a hyper-connected world, the rhythm of progress is set by those who not only know but also effectively manage what they know. For young professionals, the ability to stand out in the crowd is no longer solely dependent on one's academic qualifications or technical prowess but on the capacity to smartly navigate, curate, and apply knowledge. The journey of understanding why Personal Knowledge Management (PKM) is paramount for the modern professional is both enlightening and transformative.

Navigating the Information Deluge

Challenges of Information Overload

The digital age, while spectacularly abundant, has its own pitfalls. The plethora of platforms, constant content updates, the barrage of notifications, and the unending streams of articles, posts, and tweets lead to a phenomenon we can aptly term as 'information fatigue'. This overwhelming tide can cause decision paralysis, reduce creativity, and even lead to burnout. Furthermore, the risk of falling prey to misinformation or getting ensnared in echo chambers is higher than ever.

PKM as a Solution

In this vast ocean of data, PKM emerges as the lighthouse, guiding young professionals to safe and productive shores. It provides a systematic approach to filter out the noise, focus on the essentials, and interact with information meaningfully. Through PKM, young professionals can curate their own information ecosystem, honing in on quality sources, organizing insights, and ensuring that their knowledge reservoir remains relevant and actionable.

Career Growth and PKM

How PKM Can Accelerate Professional Development

In a rapidly evolving professional landscape, the shelf-life of specific skills is shrinking. However, the ability to continuously learn, adapt, and apply knowledge can set an individual apart. PKM promotes proactive learning and encourages professionals to stay ahead of industry curves. By consolidating learning resources, reflecting on experiences, and making conscious efforts to connect the dots between seemingly disparate pieces of information, young professionals can foster innovation and position themselves as thought leaders in their fields.

PKM as a Lifelong Learning Tool

Life is a continuum of learning, and the boundaries between formal education and self-driven learning are blurring. PKM serves as an anchor in this continuum. It's more than a one-off strategy; it's a lifelong companion. As young professionals evolve in their careers, their knowledge management strategies can grow with them, ensuring they always have a pulse on the insights that matter most. Whether it's about pivoting to a new industry, leading a team, or starting an entrepreneurial venture, PKM offers the framework to keep learning and growing.

Connecting with the Digital Generation

How Young Professionals Relate to Digital Tools

For the generation that has grown up swiping, clicking, and navigating the digital maze, online platforms are second nature. They don't just use digital tools—they resonate with them. Whether it's the instinct to Google a query, the impulse to share an insight on LinkedIn, or the habit of diving into a podcast during commutes, young professionals have seamlessly integrated digital tools into their daily routines.

Harnessing Digital Tools for PKM

Given this innate comfort with the digital realm, young professionals are perfectly poised to leverage these tools for enhanced knowledge management. From AI-driven note-taking apps that can summarize lengthy articles to social media platforms that can be transformed into learning communities, the possibilities are endless. By consciously channeling their digital interactions towards systematic knowledge management, young professionals can turn their everyday digital engagements into rich, learning experiences.

In essence, the symbiotic relationship between young professionals and PKM is undeniable. As they venture into the vast expanse of the professional world, their PKM strategies will be their compass, their anchor, and their guiding star. Embracing PKM is not just about managing knowledge—it's about sculpting a unique professional identity in the digital age.

Roadmap for the Book

As you embark on this enlightening journey of mastering Personal Knowledge Management (PKM), having a clear roadmap will enhance your understanding and application of the concepts. This section serves as your compass, offering you a succinct glimpse into the expanse of the landscape we are about to traverse.

Overview of Chapters

Chapter 1: The Digital Knowledge Revolution
Delve deep into the dramatic shift in the way knowledge is created, shared, and consumed in our digital age. Explore the transformative effects of this revolution on both individuals and societies at large.

Chapter 2: Understanding Personal Knowledge Management
Unravel the core concepts of PKM. This chapter lays the foundation, exploring the nuances, significance, and evolution of PKM in contemporary settings.

Chapter 3: The Foundations of PKM
Before diving into the nitty gritty, it's essential to grasp the underlying principles and philosophies that guide effective PKM practices.

Chapter 4: Tools of the Trade
A practical dive into the array of digital and analog tools available for PKM. From note-taking apps to advanced AI-driven platforms, discover the myriad ways to organize your knowledge.

Chapter 5: Building Your Personal Knowledge System
Learn the intricacies of creating a cohesive, personalized system that aligns with your learning style, career goals, and aspirations.

Chapter 6: Curating and Filtering Information
With the information deluge of the digital age, discerning and selecting what to absorb is crucial. This chapter will guide you on how to stay focused amidst the noise.

Chapter 7: Transforming Knowledge into Action
Knowledge without application is like a dormant seed. Explore strategies to ensure that your accumulated wisdom translates into tangible results.

Chapter 8: Sharing and Collaborating
In the age of connectivity, knowledge flourishes through sharing and collaboration. Understand the dynamics of collective wisdom and how to contribute effectively.

Chapter 9: Overcoming PKM Challenges
Every system has its hurdles. This chapter delves into potential pitfalls and offers insights on navigating them with grace and efficiency.

Chapter 10: PKM for Career Advancement
Witness the power of PKM in propelling your professional trajectory, with real-world examples and actionable strategies.

Chapter 11: PKM for Entrepreneurs
For the innovators and trailblazers, this chapter is tailored to show how PKM can be a game-changer in the entrepreneurial realm.

Conclusion: Reflecting on the PKM Journey and Envisioning the Future
As our exploration draws to a close, we'll ponder on the transformative journey of PKM and look ahead to the exciting potentials of the future.

Appendices: Supplementary Tools and Insights for Your PKM Journey
Additional resources, case studies, and tools to further enrich your PKM practices.

What to Expect

Throughout this guide, anticipate a harmonious blend of theory, real-world examples, actionable strategies, and reflective exercises. This isn't just a book; it's an interactive journey designed to reshape the way you perceive, manage, and leverage knowledge.

Who Can Benefit from This Book

While the primary audience is young professionals, the principles and strategies of PKM are universal. Whether you're a student gearing up for the professional world, a seasoned executive looking for an edge, or a lifelong learner passionate about optimizing knowledge, there's a treasure trove of insights waiting for you.

Let the journey begin. Embrace the wisdom, strategies, and practices laid out in these chapters, and you'll emerge not just informed, but transformed. Welcome to the universe of Personal Knowledge Management.

Getting Started with PKM

Amidst the cacophony of the digital age, where every click brings forth a cascade of information, the art and science of Personal Knowledge Management (PKM) can be your sanctuary. Like all journeys, setting out on the path of PKM demands preparation, the right equipment, and most importantly, the right mindset. As you prepare to embark on this enlightening voyage, this guide is your first step.

Preparing for Your PKM Journey

Assessing Your Current Knowledge Management Practices
Before diving into the world of PKM, it's essential to take stock of where you stand. Reflect on how you currently manage information. Do you often find yourself overwhelmed with excess data? Do valuable insights get lost in the chaos? By understanding your present habits, strengths, and areas of improvement, you create a baseline from which to evolve.

Setting Personal Goals for PKM
PKM isn't a one-size-fits-all solution; it's a personalized experience. Defining what you hope to achieve—whether it's staying updated in your professional field, cultivating a new hobby, or simply enhancing your daily productivity—will guide your PKM strategies and techniques.

Tools and Technologies

Introduction to PKM Tools and Software
In our digital era, an array of tools and platforms are designed to aid in knowledge management. From digital note-taking apps like Evernote and Notion to sophisticated AI-driven platforms that predict and curate content, the options are vast. Familiarize yourself with the spectrum of available tools, their features, and their potential applications.

Choosing the Right Tools for You
The allure of shiny new tools can be tempting, but remember: the best tool is the one you'll use consistently. Reflect on your personal and professional

needs, your comfort with technology, and your long-term goals. You might find that a combination of digital tools and traditional methods, like journaling, best suits your style.

Building a PKM Mindset

The Importance of Curiosity and Continuous Learning
At its core, PKM thrives on curiosity. It's the burning questions, the urge to delve deeper, and the passion for continuous learning that drive successful PKM practices. By nurturing a naturally inquisitive mindset, you pave the way for richer and more meaningful engagements with information.

Cultivating Information Literacy
In an age where the line between fact and fiction can often blur, information literacy becomes paramount. It's not just about accessing information but discerning its validity, relevance, and bias. Equip yourself with the skills to critically evaluate sources, understand contexts, and differentiate between quality content and mere noise.

As you set forth on this PKM journey, remember: it's an ongoing process of evolution. There will be moments of clarity and instances of confusion, but with every step, you're crafting a unique knowledge landscape that resonates with your goals, passions, and aspirations. Welcome to the transformative world of Personal Knowledge Management.

Chapter 1:

The Digital Knowledge Revolution

The Digital Knowledge Revolution has become the lifeblood of the 21st century. Amid the din of smartphones, broadband connections, and wireless networks, we find ourselves in the midst of an era that is unprecedented in terms of the sheer volume and accessibility of information. The significance of this change can't be overstated, especially for young professionals who are tasked with not only navigating this expansive digital ocean but also harnessing its power to achieve their professional and personal goals.

To appreciate the depth and breadth of the digital revolution, it's important to first understand the journey of knowledge sharing throughout history. Millennia ago, knowledge was passed down orally, with stories, teachings, and traditions whispered from one generation to the next. The invention of the printing press in the 15th century was a monumental leap, making books and thus knowledge, more widely available. Libraries started to flourish, and for the first time, masses had access to the knowledge that was once reserved for the elite.

But then came the 20th century, and with it, a series of technological innovations that paved the way for today's digital age. Computers, the internet, smartphones - each of these played a pivotal role in transitioning society into a new paradigm of knowledge dissemination. The pace was so rapid that what took hundreds of years in the past was now being condensed into mere decades.

Defining the digital revolution isn't merely about listing the gadgets or technologies. It's about understanding its profound characteristics. Firstly, the immediacy of information stands out. Today, we have real-time access to global news, academic research, cultural content, and more, all at our fingertips. Gone are the days when we had to wait for tomorrow's newspaper or a monthly journal to update ourselves. Secondly, there's the democratization of knowledge. The digital age has been a great equalizer, allowing anyone, irrespective of their background, to create, share, and consume content. From blogging platforms to self-publishing tools, the barriers to entry have been significantly lowered. Thirdly, the scope of the digital revolution is truly global. The interconnected nature of the internet has given rise to a universal culture of knowledge-sharing where boundaries of nation, language, and culture are becoming increasingly porous.

The impact of the digital revolution, especially for young professionals, has been both exhilarating and overwhelming. On the one hand, there's an empowering sense of having the world's knowledge in one's pocket. On the other, the challenge of discerning relevant information from the incessant digital chatter becomes paramount. The digital age demands not just passive consumption, but an active engagement with information, a skill that becomes critical for success.

In the subsequent chapters, we'll dive deep into the nuances of Personal Knowledge Management (PKM), offering young professionals a roadmap to mastering knowledge in this digital age. But for now, let's take a moment to marvel at the era we find ourselves in - a time of boundless potential and unprecedented access to knowledge. And remember, in this age, it's not about knowing everything; it's about knowing how to navigate the vast sea of everything.

The Transition from Traditional to Digital Knowledge
The evolution of knowledge dissemination over the ages is nothing short of fascinating. We've journeyed from inscriptions on cave walls to the weightless bytes of the internet, and each phase in this transition has uniquely shaped the way we learn, share, and build upon existing knowledge.

In the predigital age, libraries were sanctuaries of knowledge. Rows upon rows of books contained information on every conceivable topic. These repositories were the primary hubs where scholars, students, and curious minds congregated. Libraries were more than mere storage spaces; they were centers of intellectual exploration and discourse. Books, with their tactile feel and irreplaceable aroma, were the primary vessels of knowledge. They were both personal and shared, allowing for annotations in the margins and passed from hand to hand, weaving a tapestry of shared human experience.

Traditional schooling, too, played an invaluable role. It was structured, with curricula designed to impart foundational knowledge across various disciplines. Classrooms were where theoretical knowledge met practical application, where debates sparked and young minds were molded. This system of formal education and its pedagogical methods stood strong for centuries, laying the groundwork for critical thinking and structured learning.

However, the last few decades of the 20th century heralded a sea change. The birth of the internet was the first in a series of transformative events. Suddenly, the world was interconnected. Information was no longer confined to physical spaces; it was digitized, making it easy to transmit and access. As the internet grew, so did the need for structured data retrieval, leading to the evolution of search engines. Google, among others, became the gateway to the world's information, allowing users to explore a topic with just a few keystrokes.

Then, with the 21st century came the rise of social media. Platforms like Facebook, Twitter, and LinkedIn provided a new paradigm of knowledge-sharing, one that was immediate and personal. No longer were people merely consumers of content; they became creators, sharing insights, experiences, and narratives in real-time.

However, among these technological leaps, the journey from static pages to dynamic knowledge truly encapsulates the essence of the digital age. Websites were no longer digital brochures; they became living, evolving entities. Wikipedia is a prime example. Instead of a single author or a small group of editors, Wikipedia handed the power of knowledge creation and validation to the masses. Articles could be edited in real time, allowing for a democratic and up-to-date sharing of information.

Blogs became the new-age journals, giving voice to millions. They offered a platform for deep dives into niche topics, personal narratives, and expert commentary, blurring the lines between professional journalists and passionate hobbyists. Podcasts, on the other hand, resurrected the age-old charm of oral storytelling but with a digital twist. They provided a space for dialogues, interviews, and stories, often bridging the gap between the expert and the layman.

The transition from traditional to digital knowledge is not merely about new platforms or technologies; it's about a fundamental shift in how we perceive, interact with, and disseminate knowledge. As we move forward, it's essential for young professionals to not just adapt but to leverage these changes, harnessing the power of digital tools while respecting the foundations laid by traditional systems.

The transition from traditional to digital knowledge is not merely about new platforms or technologies; it's about a fundamental shift in how we perceive, interact with, and disseminate knowledge. A significant hallmark of this transformation has been the democratization of knowledge production and dissemination. In the predigital era, producing and sharing knowledge was often confined to a select few—authors, scholars, educators. There was an inherent gate keeping mechanism, often based on academic pedigree, access to publishing resources, or societal status.

However, the digital age has upended this model. Today, anyone with an internet connection can produce content, share insights, and contribute to the global knowledge pool. Bloggers from remote parts of the world can influence global discourse; amateur historians can curate digital exhibitions; students can create tutorial videos that garner millions of views. The power dynamics have shifted from centralized institutions to decentralized networks of individuals. This democratization has led to a richer, more diverse tapestry of perspectives and narratives, allowing for a more inclusive and holistic understanding of topics.

While this democratization has its myriad benefits, it also brings forth challenges. The sheer volume of information and the blurred lines between expert-led and user-generated content necessitate critical thinking and discernment. However, one thing is certain: knowledge is no longer the privilege of the few but the right of the many.

As we move forward, it's essential for young professionals to not just adapt but to leverage these changes. They must harness the power of digital tools, respect the foundations laid by traditional systems, and actively participate in the democratic process of knowledge creation and sharing, ensuring that the digital age continues to be one of enlightenment and growth.

Digital Natives and the New Learning Paradigm
The transformation of the knowledge landscape has given rise to distinct generational experiences, forging a chasm between those who were born into the digital age and those who witnessed its dawning and had to adapt. These two groups, termed "digital natives" and "digital immigrants," represent the changing dynamics of how knowledge is consumed, processed, and integrated into our daily lives.

"Digital natives" is a term coined to describe individuals who have grown up in the age of the internet. For these individuals, digital technologies are not mere tools but integral facets of their everyday existence. They've never known a world without internet connectivity, smartphones, or social media. Their innate understanding of digital interfaces, often taken for granted, stems from a lifetime of immersion in a world where digital and physical realities seamlessly intertwine. Information has always been a few clicks away, friendships solidified through online interactions, and entertainment sourced from virtual realms.

In stark contrast stand the "digital immigrants," those who were born before the digital age and had to migrate into this new technological landscape. This group has experienced the transformative journey from rotary phones to smartphones, from library card catalogs to digital databases, and from hand-written letters to instant messaging. While many digital immigrants have adeptly adapted to the modern tech-scape, their approach often carries remnants of the analog world. This generational gap in technology adaptation has profound implications. Digital immigrants might exhibit a learning curve with new platforms or express hesitancy with emerging digital trends, which can lead to feelings of estrangement or even techno phobia.

However, it's not merely about who can use an iPad without a manual or who feels more comfortable with a paper book. This divide symbolizes a shift in the learning paradigm itself. The rise of the internet has democratized access to knowledge in ways unimaginable just a few decades ago. Traditional classrooms and lecture halls, while still vital, are now complemented by a vast digital universe of learning resources.

Online courses, from platforms like Coursera or Udemy, have made it possible for someone in a remote village to access lectures from esteemed professors at Ivy League institutions. Massive Open Online Courses (MOOCs), such as those offered by edX or Khan Academy, provide high-quality education to anyone, anywhere, often free of charge. Beyond structured courses, platforms like YouTube have revolutionized the tutorial landscape. Whether one wishes to understand quantum physics, master a software program, or even learn to cook a new dish, there's likely a YouTube video explaining it.

In this evolved landscape, self-directed learning reigns supreme. Digital natives, especially, exhibit a propensity for seeking knowledge on-demand, driven by curiosity, immediate needs, or professional aspirations. They're not waiting for formal courses or workshops; they're Googling, watching, and experimenting in real-time.

For young professionals today, especially digital natives, this means unprecedented opportunities but also novel challenges. The ability to discern reliable sources, to stay self-motivated in an age of distractions, and to continuously adapt to ever-evolving digital tools becomes paramount. As we journey deeper into the digital age, the lines between native and immigrant might blur, but the essence remains: a world where learning is boundless, dynamic, and at the fingertips of the curious.

The Double-edged Sword of Information Abundance

The contemporary era, often dubbed the "Information Age," is defined by an abundance of digital content. Every day, petabytes of data are added to the vast digital universe, ranging from scholarly articles and news reports to personal blogs, tweets, and Instagram stories. This proliferation, fueled by the democratization of content creation and the accessibility of digital platforms, represents both a boon and a bane for society at large.

The exponential growth of digital content is staggering. Every minute, users upload hours of video content on YouTube, share thousands of photos on Instagram, and send millions of tweets. Websites mushroom daily, each adding to the immense repository of information available at our fingertips. Such growth would have been inconceivable in the pre-internet era, where information production and dissemination were largely confined to a select group of institutions and individuals.

This abundance brings with it manifold benefits. Firstly, the diversity of perspectives has never been greater. Gone are the days when a few gatekeepers decided what was newsworthy or relevant. Today, narratives from every corner of the globe, from myriad cultures and subcultures, contribute to a rich tapestry of global discourse. This inclusivity, while not without its challenges, provides a more holistic view of global events and issues.

Another advantage lies in the speed at which information can be updated. In a dynamic world, where situations evolve rapidly, digital platforms offer real-time insights, ensuring that individuals and institutions can make decisions based on the most recent data. Furthermore, the accessibility afforded by the digital age is unparalleled. Whether you're a student in New York or a farmer in a remote village in India, the internet offers a treasure trove of information, often free of charge or at minimal cost.

However, the flip side of this abundance is a landscape riddled with challenges. Among the most pressing issues is the proliferation of misinformation. The ease with which content can be created and shared means that false narratives, intentionally or unintentionally, can spread like wildfire. In an age where sensationalism often trumps accuracy, discerning fact from fiction becomes a crucial skill.

Moreover, the sheer volume of content has inadvertently contributed to dwindling attention spans. The constant barrage of notifications, updates, and feeds means that many are skimming rather than deeply engaging with content. This trend poses challenges not just for individual comprehension but for societies that rely on well-informed citizens.

Lastly, the vastness of available information can lead to "analysis paralysis." With so many sources, opinions, and data points, individuals can find themselves overwhelmed, unable to make decisions or form opinions. This cognitive overload, while a testament to the riches of the digital age, requires new strategies for information management and consumption.

In essence, the abundance of information in the digital age is a double-edged sword. It offers opportunities for learning, growth, and connection like never before, but it also demands vigilance, discernment, and adaptability. As we continue to navigate this intricate landscape, striking a balance between embracing the benefits and mitigating the challenges becomes the clarion call for all digital denizens.

The Challenges of Information Overload for Digital Natives

While the digital age has heralded unprecedented access to information, it has simultaneously ushered in a new set of challenges, particularly for digital natives. For those who've grown up in this era of boundless data and constant connectivity, the repercussions of information overload manifest in both cognitive and emotional spheres, influencing how they learn, interact, and even perceive the world around them.

From a cognitive standpoint, the inundation of digital stimuli can have profound implications. Memory, once the bedrock of learning, is being re calibrated. Why memorize facts when they are a quick search away? Yet, this reliance on external digital memory may affect our ability to internalize and synthesize information. Attention, too, has become a scarce commodity. In a world rife with notifications, pop-ups, and incessant updates, maintaining sustained attention on a single task has become an uphill battle for many. This continuous partial attention can, in turn, impact decision-making. With a plethora of choices and stimuli, the cognitive load can result in rushed or even paralyzed decision processes.

Emotionally, the deluge of digital content presents its own set of challenges. Anxiety levels, especially among younger individuals, have seen a surge. This is, in part, due to the constant barrage of information, making it difficult to switch off or disengage. There's also the pervasive FOMO, or Fear of Missing Out, a phenomenon where individuals, especially on social media platforms, feel an incessant need to stay updated, fearing they might miss out on something important or trending. This can lead to compulsive behaviors, with many incessantly checking their devices. As a result, the quest for a "digital detox" – a break from digital devices and online platforms – has gained momentum, signaling a collective yearning to reconnect with the tangible and real, away from the digital onslaught.

In the realm of learning, the paradox of choice comes into sharp focus. With countless courses, tutorials, and resources available, the ability to choose becomes both a gift and a curse. While on one hand, learners have an extensive range of topics at their disposal, on the other, they may find themselves overwhelmed, unable to select a path or stick to one. This abundance can lead to a jack-of-all-trades scenario, where individuals have a superficial understanding of many topics but mastery of none.

This brings us to the pivotal challenge of balancing depth versus breadth. The current digital environment, with its quick reads, bite-sized videos, and flashy info graphics, encourages skimming the surface. While this allows for a broad understanding, it often comes at the cost of depth.

However, true expertise, innovation, and profound insights often arise from deep dives into subjects. For digital natives, recognizing the importance of delving deep, of dedicating time to truly understand and master a topic, becomes crucial.

In conclusion, while the digital age offers digital natives a world of opportunities, it also presents unique challenges. Navigating these requires a blend of self-awareness, critical thinking, and, at times, conscious disengagement. By recognizing the implications of information overload and actively seeking balance, digital natives can harness the power of the digital age while safeguarding their cognitive and emotional well-being.

The digital knowledge revolution, as we've traversed in this chapter, is undeniably one of the most transformative phenomena of our era. It has redefined how we consume, produce, and share knowledge, bridging gaps and forging connections like never before. For the young professional, especially the digital native, this revolution offers a playground of opportunities, a canvas broadened by technology's touch, where learning is no longer confined by walls, and knowledge knows no boundaries.
Yet, as with any monumental shift, this revolution is not without its shadows. The pitfalls of information abundance, the emotional and cognitive challenges of the digital deluge, and the intricate dance of depth versus breadth all paint a complex picture. The same tools that empower can also overwhelm. The same platforms that enlighten can also mislead.

So, where does this leave the ambitious, curious, and determined young professional of today? How does one harness the vastness of the digital realm without being consumed by it? How does one remain grounded in a world that's constantly in flux?

The answer, as we'll explore in the chapters ahead, lies in a powerful approach: Personal Knowledge Management (PKM). PKM is not just a set of tools or techniques; it's a philosophy, a mindset geared towards navigating the intricacies of the digital age. It's about curating, synthesizing, and applying knowledge in ways that align with one's personal and professional goals.

As we delve deeper, we'll unpack the tenets of PKM, offering insights and strategies to not just survive but thrive in this digital age. The journey ahead is about empowerment, about crafting a personalized compass that points the way amidst the digital storm. The digital knowledge revolution has set the stage. Now, it's time to master the art of navigating it. Stay with us. The future beckons.

Chapter 2:

Understanding Personal Knowledge Management (PKM)

Defining Personal Knowledge Management

The digital age, with its information deluge, demands not just passive consumption but active curation and discerning application. As we grapple with the challenges of information overload, the importance of managing what we know—and how we know it—becomes paramount. Enter Personal Knowledge Management, or PKM, a systematic approach to navigating the vast seas of information that flood our daily lives.

Before delving deeper, it's pivotal to clarify certain terms that often get used interchangeably but have distinct nuances: "knowledge" and "information."

At its core, "information" refers to data points—facts, figures, or statements that exist in isolation. It's the raw material, so to speak. When you read a news article, browse a statistic, or glance at a notification, you are interacting with information. It's everywhere, and in the digital age, it's abundant, often to the point of being overwhelming.

"Knowledge," on the other hand, is what happens when information is processed, contextualized, and internalized. It's information that has been made meaningful. When we relate information to what we already know, reflect upon it, and integrate it into our understanding, we transform it into knowledge. Knowledge, therefore, is both personal and transformative. It's not just about what you know but how you connect and apply what you know.

With these distinctions in mind, we can now approach PKM in its essence. Personal Knowledge Management isn't about hoarding every piece of information we come across. Instead, it's about selectively capturing information that resonates or holds value for us. It's about sifting through the noise to find the signals, the nuggets of wisdom that can enrich our personal or professional lives.

But capturing is just the first step. Once we have this information, PKM emphasizes organizing it in a way that's meaningful and accessible. This could mean categorizing insights based on themes, using digital tools to store and retrieve data, or creating visual maps to link related ideas. The organization is not a one-size-fits-all; what matters is that it aligns with an individual's thinking and retrieval processes.

Lastly, and perhaps most importantly, PKM underscores the application of knowledge. Knowledge that isn't applied remains dormant and loses its potential impact. Whether it's leveraging insights in a work project, integrating them into daily life, or sharing them with others, the real power of PKM shines when knowledge is set into motion.

In essence, Personal Knowledge Management is a beacon in the bustling bazaar of the digital age. It's a tool, a philosophy, and a strategy, guiding us in capturing the valuable, organizing the meaningful, and applying the transformative. As we journey further into this chapter, we'll explore the nuances, tools, and techniques that make PKM the quintessential skill for the modern age.

Historical Evolution of PKM
Personal Knowledge Management, though sounding decidedly modern, is deeply rooted in human history. Long before digital devices, cloud storage, or AI-driven tools, our ancestors grappled with the need to manage their knowledge efficiently, weaving intricate systems and strategies to aid memory, understanding, and application.

Early Precursors:
The art of memory, or the "ars memoriae," traces back to ancient civilizations. One of the most fascinating methods was the Memory

Palace, or the "Method of Loci." Stemming from ancient Greek and Roman times, this technique hinged on associating information with distinct, vivid locations within a familiar spatial environment, such as a palace or one's home. By walking through this space mentally, one could retrieve information with ease. This was not merely a mnemonic trick but an early form of knowledge management, as it organized and prioritized information based on spatial associations.

Note-taking, too, is a time-honored tradition. Thinkers, writers, and scholars have long kept notebooks and journals to capture insights, observations, and reflections. Leonardo da Vinci's elaborate notebooks, filled with sketches, observations, and inventions, are a testament to the age-old human urge to record and organize knowledge. These pre-digital systems, while rudimentary compared to today's tools, underscore a timeless human need: to manage and make sense of the knowledge we accumulate.

The Influence of Technology:
As we transitioned into the 20th century, technology began playing a pivotal role in how we managed knowledge. Early computers and desktop databases allowed individuals to store, categorize, and retrieve information more efficiently than paper-based systems. These digital tools, though limited in capacity and reach by today's standards, marked the beginning of a shift towards more systematic, scalable, and versatile knowledge management.

The advent of the internet, and later cloud storage, further transformed PKM. No longer were individuals confined to their local storage or physical notebooks. Information could be saved, accessed, and shared from anywhere, anytime. Collaborative tools, like wikis and shared documents, allowed for cooperative knowledge creation and management, breaking down barriers of geography and time zones.

The Rise of PKM in the Digital Age:
The digital age, with its explosion of content—blogs, videos, podcasts, courses, and more—brought along an urgent need for discerning curation.

While early PKM systems focused primarily on storage and retrieval, the modern PKM approach intertwines with curation, synthesis, and application.

As every individual became both a consumer and a producer of content, the lines between personal and shared knowledge blurred. The interplay between growing digital content and the need for personal curation was the fertile ground from which contemporary PKM sprouted. It became less about merely storing information and more about weaving a personal tapestry of knowledge, discerning the valuable from the trivial, and building bridges between disparate pieces of information.

In sum, while the tools, methods, and scale have evolved, the essence of PKM remains rooted in a timeless quest: to navigate, understand, and leverage the vast landscapes of knowledge. From ancient memory palaces to modern cloud databases, this journey of PKM reflects humanity's enduring aspiration to master the realm of the known and the unknown.

Components and Processes of PKM
PKM isn't just about tools or isolated techniques. It's a holistic process, a cyclical journey of interacting with information and knowledge throughout various stages of one's professional and personal life. Breaking down this intricate dance, we identify four pivotal components that form the PKM lifecycle. These steps, though outlined sequentially, often overlap and loop back, reflecting the dynamic nature of knowledge in the digital age.

The PKM Lifecycle: From Knowledge Acquisition to Application

Seeking:
The very onset of the PKM journey lies in the act of seeking. It's about curiosity-driven exploration, about diving into the vast digital oceans to locate and access relevant knowledge. This could mean sifting through articles on a topic, scouting for educational videos, or joining online forums and groups related to one's interests. In this age, with an overwhelming amount of information available, seeking isn't just about finding; it's about discerning. It's about differentiating the valuable from the noise, and filtering content that aligns with one's goals or needs.

Sense-making:

Once knowledge has been sought, the next step is to process and make sense of it. Sense-making involves reflecting on the acquired information, comparing it with what one already knows, and piecing together a coherent understanding. It might mean synthesizing insights from multiple sources, identifying patterns, or drawing inferences. Contextualizing the information, relating it to real-world scenarios or one's personal experiences, is vital at this stage. Sense-making breathes life into raw information, transforming it into usable, actionable knowledge.

Sharing:

Knowledge, once made sense of, yearns to be shared. In the digital age, sharing isn't just about dissemination but also about contribution and collaboration. Whether it's posting insights on a personal blog, engaging in online discussions, or collaborating on shared platforms, sharing serves dual purposes. Firstly, it reinforces one's understanding, as teaching or discussing often crystallizes knowledge. Secondly, it contributes to the broader community, fostering a culture of collective learning. In the PKM lifecycle, sharing is the bridge between personal understanding and communal growth.

Storing:

The final step, but by no means the least, is storing. Knowledge, if not archived or organized, can easily dissipate in the mists of memory or get lost in the digital clutter. Storing is about creating a structured repository, a personal library of sorts, where knowledge can be easily retrieved when needed. This could mean using digital tools like note-taking apps, databases, or cloud storage. The key here is to categorize and tag information in ways that resonate with one's retrieval patterns. Storing ensures that the efforts expended in seeking and sense-making aren't short-lived but serve one in the long run.

In encapsulating the PKM lifecycle, one realizes that knowledge management isn't a linear, one-off task. It's a continual process, a rhythmic dance of seeking, processing, sharing, and archiving. As the digital landscape evolves, and as one's personal and professional goals shift, the

PKM lifecycle adapts, ensuring that knowledge remains a dynamic, living entity, always ready to serve and enrich.

The Tangible Benefits of Effective PKM
Embracing Personal Knowledge Management is not merely an intellectual exercise or a trend to jump on. It offers tangible, palpable benefits that can transform the way we work, learn, and grow in the digital age. The merits of effective PKM stretch beyond just "knowing more." They ripple into various facets of our lives, enhancing our capacity, agility, and impact in a world that never stops evolving.

Enhancing Decision-making:
In the professional world, decision-making stands as a cornerstone of success. Whether it's charting a new business strategy, selecting a technological solution, or navigating team dynamics, decisions shape trajectories. Effective PKM plays a pivotal role here. By having a well-organized repository of personal knowledge, professionals can tap into relevant insights, past experiences, and contextual understandings with ease. This empowers them to make informed decisions, backed not just by external data but also by internalized knowledge. In essence, PKM serves as a compass, guiding individuals towards choices that align with both objective realities and personal convictions.

Boosting Productivity:
We've all been there — wading through digital files, revisiting countless websites, or rummaging through notes, just to locate that one piece of information we need. In a scattered information environment, precious time and energy are often expended on searching for or recreating knowledge. Effective PKM drastically reduces this friction. With a structured, intuitive system in place, retrieving knowledge becomes seamless. Information is at one's fingertips, ready to be leveraged when needed. This boosts productivity, ensuring that efforts are directed towards creation, innovation, and application rather than redundant searches or recreations.

Continuous Learning and Adaptation:
The digital age is synonymous with rapid change. Technologies evolve, paradigms shift, and what was relevant yesterday might become obsolete tomorrow. In such a landscape, continuous learning isn't just an asset; it's a necessity. PKM, with its emphasis on seeking and sense-making, fosters a culture of perpetual learning. It instills a habit of curiosity, of consistently updating one's knowledge base. Moreover, as one organizes and shares this newly acquired knowledge, the learning gets reinforced. PKM, therefore, acts as a scaffold, supporting individuals in keeping pace with the fast-evolving digital world. It ensures that they aren't just passive consumers of change but active participants, adapting and thriving amidst flux.

In concluding this section, it becomes evident that the benefits of PKM aren't confined to the cerebral realm. They manifest in tangible, impactful ways, enriching our professional endeavors, optimizing our time, and ensuring that we remain agile learners in a world that's in perennial motion. Adopting PKM isn't just about managing knowledge; it's about harnessing its power to lead, innovate, and flourish.

PKM and Personal Growth
Personal Knowledge Management, while rooted in the domain of knowledge and learning, has profound implications for personal development. Its tentacles extend into the realms of mindset, branding, and interpersonal dynamics, acting as a catalyst for holistic growth. When integrated effectively, PKM becomes more than just a method; it transforms into a life philosophy, reshaping our approach to learning, contribution, and relationships.

Fostering a Growth Mindset:
The very core of PKM revolves around the continuous acquisition, processing, and application of knowledge. It instills a belief that learning is not static, confined to classrooms or specific life phases, but an ongoing journey. This aligns perfectly with Dr. Carol Dweck's concept of the "growth mindset" — the belief that abilities and intelligence can be developed through dedication and hard work. By actively seeking out information, reflecting upon it, and integrating it into our knowledge base,

PKM naturally cultivates this growth-oriented perspective. Over time, this mindset becomes a driving force, propelling individuals towards continuous self-improvement, resilience in the face of challenges, and a hunger for learning in all spheres of life.

Building a Personal Brand:
In today's digital age, personal branding is not just for celebrities or public figures. Everyone has a unique blend of experiences, knowledge, and insights that can be shared, and PKM plays an instrumental role in this. By consistently sharing and contributing knowledge, whether through blogs, social media, webinars, or discussions, individuals position themselves as thought leaders in specific domains. Over time, this creates a reputation, a personal brand, where they are recognized and sought after for their expertise. PKM, in essence, provides the raw material and the framework for this branding, enabling individuals to carve out a niche for themselves in the vast digital landscape.

Strengthening Interpersonal Relationships:
Knowledge, when leveraged effectively, can be a bridge, connecting individuals in collaborative endeavors. PKM equips individuals with a rich reservoir of insights that can be brought to the table in team settings, collaborative projects, or even casual discussions. By adding value through knowledge, individuals can foster stronger interpersonal relationships. They become assets in team scenarios, offering solutions, perspectives, or insights drawn from their personal knowledge repositories. Moreover, the act of sharing knowledge fosters trust, respect, and mutual growth, weaving stronger bonds in professional and personal circles.

PKM transcends the boundaries of mere knowledge management to become a beacon for personal growth. It shapes mindsets, crafts reputations, and enhances relationships, ensuring that the individual doesn't just grow in knowledge, but in character, influence, and impact. In embracing PKM, one doesn't just navigate the digital age better; one evolves as a more enlightened, empowered, and connected being.

PKM and Career Advancement

The modern career landscape is more fluid and dynamic than ever, influenced by technological advancements, evolving industry needs, and the ever-present hum of the global market. Amidst these shifts, PKM emerges as a powerful ally, aligning one's personal growth with career aspirations, and ensuring that professionals remain not just relevant, but indispensable in their chosen fields. The influence of PKM on career advancement can be seen through strategic planning, networking opportunities, and real-world success stories.

The Role of PKM in Career Planning and Strategizing:

In the intricate chess game that is career planning, PKM serves as both the board and the pieces, providing context and facilitating moves. It allows professionals to stay updated with industry trends, skills in demand, and emerging opportunities. By systematically seeking and storing such knowledge, professionals can forecast where their industry is headed and tailor their learning and skill acquisition accordingly. Furthermore, PKM aids in introspection, helping individuals recognize their strengths, gaps in their knowledge, and areas of passion. Such clarity aids in strategic career moves, be it switching roles, pursuing further education, or even transitioning into entirely new fields.

Networking and Mentorship:

It's often said that in the professional world, it's not just what you know but who you know. PKM amplifies both facets. By actively sharing knowledge — be it through industry forums, seminars, or social media — professionals invariably draw the attention of peers, industry leaders, and potential mentors. This not only expands their professional network but also opens doors for meaningful mentorship opportunities. A robust PKM system can also be a talking point in conversations, demonstrating a commitment to continuous learning and the proactive management of one's career. In networking events or interviews, referencing a personal knowledge system can set one apart, showcasing foresight, initiative, and an organized mind.

Case Studies:

Sarah, a marketing executive, consistently leveraged her PKM system to document emerging trends in consumer behavior. Over time, her insights became invaluable in her company's strategy meetings, leading her to a senior role in market analytics.

Javier, an IT professional, curated a blog as part of his PKM where he dissected complex tech topics into layman's terms. His ability to simplify and convey intricate subjects caught the eye of a major tech firm's HR, landing him a role in technical communications.

Priya, an architect, used her PKM to bridge traditional architectural methods with emerging sustainable technologies. By sharing her integrated insights on global platforms, she was soon recognized as an expert in sustainable architecture, leading to international consultancy opportunities.

These professionals, among many others, underscore the potency of PKM in career advancement. They demonstrate how the systematic acquisition, organization, and application of knowledge can shape trajectories, opening doors and creating opportunities that might have otherwise remained obscured.

To encapsulate, PKM isn't just a personal endeavor; its ripples are felt profoundly in the professional sphere. It becomes a compass, guiding professionals through the tumultuous seas of career progression, ensuring they chart courses that are informed, strategic, and aligned with both personal passion and market demands.

As we draw the curtains on this exploration of Personal Knowledge Management, a few truths emerge, clear and resonant. In the digital age, where information is abundant but true knowledge remains a treasured rarity, PKM emerges not just as a technique but as a vital life skill. It serves as a beacon, illuminating paths of personal growth, professional advancement, and holistic evolution.

The depth of PKM is seen in its intricate processes - seeking, sense-making, sharing, and storing. Each step is a journey in itself, inviting introspection, proactive learning, and mindful contribution. Its breadth, on the other hand, is evidenced in its wide-ranging impact, influencing everything from the sharpening of a growth mindset to the strategic maneuvers in a professional career.

However, like all tools, the efficacy of PKM is shaped by its user. As we've journeyed through its facets, it becomes imperative for readers to pause and reflect: Where do I stand in my PKM journey? What systems and habits have I already instituted? Where do gaps emerge, and how can I bridge them?

It's a call not just for passive understanding but active integration. The digital age is unrelenting in its pace and demands, but with PKM, each one of us holds the power to not just navigate but master this complex landscape. It equips us to transform torrents of information into streams of actionable knowledge, to find clarity amidst chaos, and to consistently evolve in a world that's in perpetual motion.

As we step into subsequent chapters, with a deeper dive into tools, techniques, and transformative stories related to PKM, it's a gentle nudge to the readers: Take this moment. Assess, reflect, and recognize. Your journey into mastering knowledge in the digital age has only just begun, and the horizons are expansive and promising.

Chapter 3:

The Foundations of PKM

Laying the Groundwork

In the quest for personal and professional evolution, understanding the nuances of Personal Knowledge Management (PKM) becomes quintessential. But before one can fully harness its power, it's crucial to lay a firm foundation, ensuring that the principles of PKM are not just superficially adopted but deeply ingrained.

Understanding the Fundamental Difference Between Just "Managing" and Truly "Mastering" Personal Knowledge:

At the heart of PKM lies a dichotomy — the difference between mere management and genuine mastery. While the former indicates a surface-level handling or controlling of information, the latter delves much deeper, signifying a profound understanding, integration, and application of the knowledge acquired.

To merely manage knowledge implies a passive approach. It's akin to hoarding books on a shelf without reading them or attending seminars without internalizing the content. The knowledge exists in one's orbit, but its real value remains untapped. Mastery, on the other hand, requires active engagement. It's about absorbing, reflecting upon, and then synthesizing what one learns into actionable insights or wisdom. Mastery implies that knowledge has not just been accumulated, but it's also been understood, contemplated, and is ready to be utilized when the situation demands.

The Intertwining of Knowledge Management with Personal Development:

As one ventures deeper into the realms of PKM, a realization emerges – knowledge management is not a soloed endeavor, distinct from the rest of one's life. Instead, it's deeply intertwined with personal development.

Every piece of knowledge we acquire, reflect upon, and apply invariably shapes us, molding our worldviews, influencing our decisions, and crafting our paths.

PKM, thus, becomes a mirror to one's evolution. It showcases one's interests, the areas they're keen to grow in, and the wisdom they've garnered over the years. As knowledge is continuously acquired and integrated, it feeds into one's personal growth, refining skills, enhancing competencies, and widening horizons.

Moreover, the very act of engaging with PKM fosters traits essential for personal development. The discipline required to seek and store knowledge, the curiosity to delve deeper, the humility to accept what one doesn't know, and the wisdom to discern relevant from redundant — all these are facets of personal growth that are honed by diligently practicing PKM.

As we lay the groundwork for a deeper dive into PKM, it's essential to recognize its holistic nature. It's not just about managing data or information but about mastering the knowledge that can transform one's life. It's about weaving together the threads of learning and personal evolution, creating a tapestry that's both enriching and enlightening. The foundations, once set, pave the way for a journey that promises growth, mastery, and endless possibilities.

The Four Pillars of PKM
Just as a building requires a strong foundation to support its weight and withstand external forces, so does Personal Knowledge Management rely on fundamental principles that form its bedrock. These principles, often referred to as the 'Four Pillars of PKM,' not only guide the processes within this domain but also ensure a comprehensive and effective approach to managing personal knowledge. They are: Aggregation, Curation, Creation, and Sharing.

Aggregation:
Aggregation is the process of gathering or collecting relevant data, information, and knowledge from various sources. In the context of PKM,

it's about actively seeking out resources, whether they be articles, books, podcasts, webinars, or even conversations, that add to one's knowledge base. This step is fundamental as it fuels the subsequent pillars, providing the raw material upon which the edifice of PKM is built.

Curation:
Once knowledge is aggregated, not all of it might be relevant, up-to-date, or even accurate. Curation steps in here, sifting through the amassed data to filter and retain only what is truly essential. It's an exercise in discernment and judgment, ensuring that one's personal knowledge repository is not just vast, but also accurate and pertinent. Curation also involves organizing this knowledge in a manner that's easily retrievable, ensuring that the insights don't get lost in the deluge.

Creation:
With a curated set of knowledge at one's disposal, the next step is to actively engage with it, leading to the creation of new insights, ideas, or perspectives. Creation in PKM doesn't merely refer to producing original content, although that's a part of it. It's about synthesis, where existing knowledge is combined, restructured, or even challenged to birth new understanding. It's a testament to the adage that knowledge isn't static but dynamic, evolving with each interaction.

Sharing:
Knowledge, when hoarded, stagnates. The fourth pillar, Sharing, ensures that knowledge flows, not just into one's repository but outwards, enriching others. Sharing can take many forms: teaching, writing, discussing, or even mentoring. It not only positions the individual as a contributor to the broader knowledge ecosystem but also reinforces their own understanding. Often, it's in the act of sharing that knowledge crystallizes, gaps are identified, and deeper insights emerge.

The Cyclical Nature of the Four Pillars:
While these pillars are presented sequentially, it's vital to understand that they aren't linear but cyclical. Sharing often leads to further aggregation as feedback and interactions bring new insights to the fore. Creation might

inspire deeper curation, ensuring that foundational knowledge supports the new insights. This cyclical interaction ensures that PKM remains a living, breathing process, constantly refreshed and rejuvenated.

In essence, these four pillars serve as guiding lights, ensuring that one's journey in PKM is not just methodical but also holistic. They ensure a balance between intake and output, reflection and action, ensuring that personal knowledge isn't just managed but truly mastered and magnified.

Aggregation: Gathering Knowledge Resources

In the vast, ever-evolving landscape of the digital age, the act of gathering knowledge is both an art and a science. It's akin to a treasure hunt, where the jewels of wisdom are scattered amidst heaps of redundant, outdated, or irrelevant information. Aggregation, the first pillar of PKM, beckons one to embark on this quest, equipped with discernment and aided by modern tools.

The Art of Seeking and Collecting Relevant Knowledge:

Aggregation is not just about hoarding every piece of information that one comes across. Instead, it's about selectively seeking out resources that resonate with one's goals, interests, and needs. It involves actively questioning the relevance, credibility, and utility of information. Every article read, podcast listened to, or webinar attended is a conscious step towards enriching one's knowledge base, making the act of aggregation as much an internal process of discernment as an external search for resources.

Tools and Strategies:

In today's digital age, a multitude of tools have emerged to aid the aggregation process, streamlining searches and ensuring that one stays updated without being overwhelmed.

RSS Feeds: Standing for "Really Simple Syndication," RSS feeds are a godsend for those seeking to keep up with their favorite blogs, news outlets, or journals. Instead of manually visiting each site, users can aggregate content into a single feed, ensuring they never miss an update.

Bookmarking Tools: Platforms like Pocket, Instapaper, or Evernote allow users to save interesting articles, videos, or web pages for later consumption. These tools often come with tagging and organizing features, making the retrieval process smoother.

Digital Libraries: Sites like Google Scholar, JSTOR, or even specific industry repositories, provide a wealth of research papers, articles, and other academic resources, aiding those looking for in-depth or specialized knowledge.

Distinguishing Signal from Noise: Finding Quality Sources Amidst Information Overload:
Perhaps the most significant challenge in aggregation is navigating the deluge of information the internet presents. Not all that glitters is gold, and in the world of online information, discerning quality content from the noise becomes paramount.

Here, a few strategies emerge:

Rely on Trusted Sources: Start with established institutions, experts in the field, or peer-reviewed journals. Over time, one can curate a list of trusted sources to frequent.

Check for Citations and References: Quality content often builds upon prior work. Articles or studies that reference their sources or provide citations can often be more credible.

Seek Diverse Perspectives: Instead of confining oneself to an echo chamber, actively seek out diverse sources and viewpoints. This not only ensures a well-rounded understanding but also mitigates the risk of misinformation.

While the act of aggregation might seem daunting given the sheer volume of information available, with the right mindset, tools, and strategies, it becomes a manageable, even enjoyable endeavor. It sets the stage for the subsequent pillars of PKM, ensuring a robust foundation of quality knowledge to curate, create, and share.

Curation: Refining and Organizing What You've Gathered
In the boundless seas of information, it's not enough to simply cast a wide net and gather; one must also refine their catch, ensuring that only the most valuable pieces remain. Curation, the second pillar of PKM, dives deep into this essential art, transforming the raw data of aggregation into a refined knowledge repository.

The Importance of Discernment and Contextualization:
Curation is not just about sorting or organizing; it's about making sense of what's been gathered. It requires discernment to differentiate between what's essential and what's not, between what's timeless and what's fleeting. Furthermore, curation also calls for contextualization, understanding not just the content itself, but also its relevance and place within the broader scope of one's knowledge.

This process helps in converting passive information into active knowledge. It's the phase where one asks probing questions, identifies gaps, challenges assumptions, and discerns patterns. It's where the seeds of insight are often sown.

Tools for Effective Curation:
In the age of digital transformation, several tools have emerged that simplify and enhance the curation process:

Digital Note-Taking Apps: Platforms like Notion, Evernote, or Microsoft OneNote allow for more than just jotting down points. They come equipped with features to categorize, link, and even collaborate on the content, turning mere notes into a dynamic knowledge base.

Tagging Systems: These allow users to categorize their collected resources effectively. Whether it's through digital bookmarking tools or dedicated knowledge databases, tagging aids in organizing and retrieving information seamlessly.

Knowledge Databases: Tools like Roam Research or Obsidian prioritize creating connections between different pieces of knowledge, facilitating the building of a personal knowledge graph. These connections often lead to deeper insights and a richer understanding of subjects.

The Balance Between Over Curation and Under Curation:
While curating is crucial, there's a delicate balance to strike. Over curation, the act of spending excessive time refining and organizing without progressing to other pillars of PKM, can become an impediment. It may lead to paralysis by analysis, where one becomes so engrossed in the curation process that they don't move forward to creation or sharing.

On the other hand, under curation risks overlooking important insights or losing valuable resources in a sea of information. The key lies in ensuring that the curation process serves its purpose: to refine and enhance knowledge without becoming an end in itself.

In wrapping up this segment on curation, it's evident that while aggregation provides the raw materials, curation molds them, giving them shape and context. It's a transformative phase in the PKM journey, turning collected data into a coherent, structured, and valuable knowledge base.

Creation: Building Upon and Personalizing Knowledge
At the heart of the PKM journey lies Creation, a pillar that transcends mere consumption to give birth to something new. Where aggregation and curation are primarily about seeking and refining, creation is the act of bringing forth, of making one's mark on the landscape of knowledge.

How Creation Solidifies and Expands Understanding:
The process of creating — be it writing, teaching, or even discussing — challenges us to crystallize our thoughts and present them coherently. By actively constructing our insights, we further embed knowledge into our psyche. Creation acts as a reinforcement mechanism, ensuring that the learned material isn't just superficially understood but deeply internalized.

Each creation becomes a testament to one's grasp over the subject. It's an external manifestation of internal comprehension, and the very act of producing it fortifies that understanding.

Translating Passive Learning into Active Application:
Consuming content is passive; it's a process of taking in. Creation, however, is active. It propels individuals beyond mere consumers to become producers, stakeholders in the vast knowledge ecosystem.

Writing: Whether it's through articles, blogs, or even personal journals, writing is a powerful mode of creation. It allows for structured thinking, elaboration, and reflection.

Projects: Tackling projects related to one's domain of interest transforms theoretical knowledge into practical application. By solving real-world problems, one validates and enriches their understanding.

Tangible Outputs: Creating models, diagrams, videos, or even software, these tangible outputs not only showcase understanding but also contribute to the broader community, becoming resources for others to learn from.

The Role of Synthesis: Merging Multiple Sources to Form New Insights: Creation isn't just about regurgitating what's been consumed. True creation often involves synthesis — the art of combining insights from multiple sources, melding them, and giving birth to something unique. This synthesis can lead to innovative ideas, new perspectives, or even the emergence of novel concepts.

By juxtaposing different viewpoints, identifying commonalities, and challenging discrepancies, synthesis allows for a richer, more nuanced view of a subject. It's where the magic of "1 + 1 = 3" happens, as the resultant insight is often greater than the sum of its parts.

Creation is where knowledge takes flight. It's where passive learning transforms into active contribution. By embracing the pillar of creation, one doesn't just solidify their understanding; they expand the boundaries of knowledge, adding their unique voice to the global chorus.

Sharing: Disseminating Knowledge and Engaging with Communities
At the frontier of the PKM journey is Sharing – the act of generously disseminating what one has learned and created, fostering connections, and engaging in enriching discussions. While the previous pillars largely focus

on personal growth, Sharing extends that growth to others, transforming personal knowledge into a collective asset.

The Two-Fold Benefits of Sharing:
The very act of sharing knowledge does wonders both for the sharer and the recipient. Firstly, as one articulates and shares their understanding with others, it reinforces their grasp over the subject. Explaining a concept to someone else, answering their queries, or even defending one's standpoint in a debate, can solidify and deepen understanding.

Secondly, by sharing, one contributes to the collective pool of knowledge. Every shared insight, every piece of advice, and every articulated thought can become a stepping stone for another's learning journey. It's a way of giving back, of ensuring that the cycle of learning, growing, and sharing continues unabated.

Platforms for Sharing:
In the digital age, myriad platforms exist that facilitate the dissemination of knowledge:

Blogs: A personal or collaborative space where one can articulate their insights, share experiences, or delve deep into specific subjects. Blogs offer a platform for both long-form content and quick musings.

Social Media: Platforms like Twitter, LinkedIn, or Instagram allow for quick sharing of thoughts, linking to resources, or engaging in discussions. They provide a vast audience and instant feedback mechanisms.

Seminars/Webinars: Physical or virtual seminars offer a structured environment for sharing. They allow for deeper dives into topics and facilitate direct engagement with an audience.

Discussions: Forums, online communities, or even informal group discussions can become powerful platforms for sharing. They foster mutual learning, challenging debates, and a sense of community.

Ethical Considerations in Sharing:
While sharing is commendable, it comes with its set of responsibilities. Ensuring ethical practices while sharing is paramount:

Crediting Sources: Whether one is quoting, paraphrasing, or building upon someone else's ideas, giving proper credit is non-negotiable. It respects the original creator and maintains the integrity of the shared content.

Respecting Privacy: Especially relevant when sharing personal experiences, case studies, or anecdotes. It's essential to ensure that no private information is divulged without consent, and any shared content doesn't harm or exploit others.

Maintaining Authenticity: Authentic sharing means being genuine, avoiding exaggerations, and staying true to one's understanding. It involves being open about what one knows, acknowledging uncertainties, and being receptive to feedback.

Sharing is the bridge between personal knowledge and collective wisdom. It's an act of generosity, a commitment to community growth, and an embodiment of the belief that knowledge, when shared, multiplies. By adhering to the ethics of sharing, one not only disseminates knowledge but also builds trust, fostering a community that thrives on mutual respect and learning.

Continuous Learning and Reflection: The Heart of PKM
In a rapidly changing world, the only constant is the unyielding march of knowledge. As new insights emerge and paradigms shift, staying still equates to moving backward. At the core of Personal Knowledge Management lies the symbiotic duo of Continuous Learning and Reflection, ensuring not just the accumulation of knowledge but its profound internalization and application.

Cultivating a Learner's Mindset in an Ever-Evolving Digital Landscape:
The digital age, marked by its incessant pace, demands a constant learner's mindset. This doesn't just mean accumulating new information; it means being adaptable, open-minded, and eternally curious. A learner's mindset

recognizes that there's always more to discover, newer perspectives to consider, and alternative methodologies to explore. It celebrates the journey of learning as much as, if not more than, the destination.

The Significance of Reflection in Internalizing and Contextualizing Knowledge:
Learning without reflection is like food without digestion. Reflection is the process of mulling over, questioning, and connecting the dots between what one knows. It gives depth to learning, ensuring that knowledge isn't just stored but understood, questioned, and synthesized. Reflection takes the raw data of learning and transforms it into wisdom, facilitating its application in varied contexts and scenarios.

Integrative Practices for Continuous Learning and Reflection:

Journaling: Putting pen to paper (or fingers to keys) and documenting one's learning journey can be immensely powerful. Journaling allows for a structured reflection, capturing moments of epiphany, challenges, questions, and progress. Over time, it becomes a chronicle of growth, a testament to one's evolving understanding.

Meditation: While often associated with spiritual or emotional well-being, meditation can also be a potent tool for reflection. Mindful meditation can provide the mental space needed to contemplate, introspect, and internalize knowledge. It fosters focus and clarity, allowing one to sift through the influx of information and discern the truly meaningful.

Feedback Loops for Self-Improvement: Constructive feedback, be it from peers, mentors, or even self-assessment, provides a mirror to one's understanding. It highlights areas of strength and pinpoints where improvement is needed. Establishing regular feedback loops ensures that the learning journey is continually calibrated, and efforts are directed where they're most beneficial.

In essence, Continuous Learning and Reflection are the heartbeat of PKM. They keep the cycle of knowledge acquisition, understanding, and application alive and thriving. In the swirling vortex of the digital age, they act as anchors, ensuring that one remains grounded in authentic understanding while soaring to new heights of knowledge. They remind us that the true essence of knowledge isn't just in knowing, but in growing.

At the heart of the edifice of Personal Knowledge Management (PKM) lies a beautiful cyclical dance, where each principle, each action, feeds into and strengthens the next. From the initial sparks of Aggregation to the nurturing touch of Curation, the innovative spirit of Creation, and the generous act of Sharing, PKM is more than just a series of steps – it's an interconnected web, where each thread reinforces the others.

The principles of PKM aren't just linear processes to be checked off a list; they're symbiotic elements in a dynamic ecosystem of personal growth. As you Aggregate, you're better informed about what to Curate. As you Curate, you discover gaps and insights that spur Creation. Creation leads to richer Sharing, which in turn exposes you to feedback and new knowledge sources to Aggregate, and the cycle continues. This continuous loop is enriched further by the overarching canopy of Continuous Learning and Reflection, ensuring depth and purpose in each phase.

For the reader stepping into or already navigating the complex terrain of the digital age, the journey of mastering personal knowledge is both a challenge and an opportunity. It's a quest marked by the allure of endless horizons of information, but also the perils of distraction, misinformation, and overload. Yet, with the compass of PKM and its foundational pillars, the path becomes clearer, the journey more purposeful.

As we wrap up our exploration of the foundational aspects of PKM, let it be a clarion call to all readers: Approach knowledge not as a mere commodity to be acquired but as a sacred entity to be revered. Engage with it with insatiable curiosity, unwavering intentionality, and a clear sense of purpose. For in the vast digital landscapes of the 21st century, it's not just about knowing more; it's about knowing better, knowing deeper, and knowing with purpose.

In this dance of knowledge, let each step be deliberate, each turn be meaningful, and may you find joy, growth, and fulfillment in every beat.

Chapter 4:
Tools of the Trade

The Digital Toolkit for Modern Knowledge Workers

In today's rapidly evolving digital landscape, the tools we employ to gather, process, and store information play a pivotal role in how effectively we harness the power of knowledge. As young professionals stepping into or growing within this age, it's crucial to not only understand but also master the use of these digital tools to manage our personal knowledge. This, in essence, is Personal Knowledge Management (PKM) for the digital age.

The past few decades have seen an exponential growth in the amount of information available at our fingertips. With this information influx, traditional methods of note-taking, organizing, and referencing, like physical notebooks and binders, are becoming less sufficient. Imagine trying to drink from a fire hydrant; that's what it feels like to process today's digital information with yesterdays tools. The amount is overwhelming, and without the right tools, it's easy to miss out on valuable knowledge or spend countless hours sifting through irrelevant data.

However, it's not about discarding the old and heralding the new unconditionally. The essence of effective PKM is in balancing modern tech capabilities with one's personal comfort and usability. Not every digital tool will suit every individual. Some might find solace in hybrid systems that combine the tangible with the digital, while others might lean fully into digital ecosystems.

The rise of digital PKM tools isn't just a result of the increasing volume of information, but also the nature of modern work and life. Workplaces have become more collaborative; projects are more dynamic, with professionals from various fields coming together to pool their expertise. As boundaries blur between disciplines, the need for a well-organized, accessible personal knowledge system becomes paramount.

Moreover, the nature of knowledge has evolved. It's no longer just about what you know; it's about how quickly and effectively you can access what you know, build upon it, and apply it in diverse contexts. Traditional methods, while comforting, may not offer the speed, flexibility, or interactivity demanded by today's professional challenges.

That said, embracing a new digital tool doesn't mean diving headfirst into the most complex system out there. The true value of a tool lies in its ability to enhance your PKM without becoming a cumbersome process in itself. As we delve into the myriad of tools available for modern knowledge workers, remember: it's about finding what complements your workflow, aligns with your objectives, and feels intuitive.

In the subsequent sections, we will explore the various digital tools designed to aid in PKM. From note-taking apps that mimic the feel of a physical notebook to sophisticated software that integrates every piece of your digital life, the array is vast and varied. Through this journey, you will discover not only the tools but also strategies to implement them effectively, ensuring that as a young professional in the digital age, you are well-equipped to ride the wave of information, rather than drown in it.

A Tour of Leading PKM Tools

Diving into the digital horizon, we find a sprawling landscape of tools designed to elevate our personal knowledge management journey. For today's young professional, this vast array presents both an opportunity and a challenge. The upside is the potential of discovering a tool tailor-made for your needs. The downside? The sheer number of options might cause a sense of overwhelm.

To navigate this expanse with clarity, let's first establish our criteria for evaluating these tools.

Criteria for Evaluating PKM Tools

Features: What functionalities does the tool bring to the table? Can it tag, link, or embed multimedia? Does it support structured hierarchy or lean more towards a free-form canvas? The features need to dovetail with your goals, be they compiling extensive research, brainstorming creative concepts, or straightforward data organization.

Usability: The tool's utility hinges on its user-friendliness. The main objective is to augment your PKM process, not introduce new hurdles. This includes a clear interface, an intuitive design, and an uncomplicated learning curve.

Scalability: As you progress, your reservoir of knowledge will inevitably grow and diversify. The tool you select should gracefully scale alongside, accommodating larger data volumes, ensuring swift search capabilities, and adapting to evolving categorization needs.

Integration Capabilities: Our digital lives span across multiple platforms and devices. A superior PKM tool can effortlessly sync with other frequently-used software, ensuring a cohesive, centralized knowledge hub and enhancing workflow fluidity.

Equipped with these benchmarks, let's delve into some of the leading PKM tools that have garnered attention and acclaim:

Notion: A versatile workspace, Notion combines note-taking, task management, databases, and more into a cohesive platform. Its drag-and-drop interface is user-friendly, and its templates can kick start your PKM journey. The tool's collaborative features also make it ideal for team projects.

Evernote: A veteran in the PKM arena, Evernote remains a favorite for many. Its strength lies in note-taking and organization, with features like tagging, notebooks, and multimedia attachments. Its web clipper feature allows users to save web pages directly to their notes.

Roam Research: Touted as a tool for "networked thought," Roam is designed for those who thrive on interconnected ideas. Its bidirectional linking system allows for the creation of a web of related notes, making it an excellent tool for researchers and writers.

Obsidian: This tool takes a local-first approach, meaning all your notes remain on your device. Like Roam, it champions linked thought, allowing you to see relationships between notes. It's also extensible with plugins, which means its capabilities can be tailored to individual needs.

Trello: For those who prefer a visual organization, Trello's board and card system is invaluable. It's especially useful for project management and task tracking. Integrations with apps like Google Drive and Slack enhance its collaborative potential.

Microsoft OneNote: A robust note-taking application, OneNote's free-form canvas allows for flexibility in organization. It supports handwriting, drawing, and multimedia embedding, making it particularly handy for tablet users.

Pocket: While primarily a read-it-later app, Pocket plays a vital role in PKM by allowing users to save articles, videos, and more from the web to revisit later. Tagging features make categorization easy.

As you acquaint yourself with these tools, always circle back to your personal and professional needs. Reflect on how each tool aligns with the criteria mentioned, and consider using them in tandem for a comprehensive PKM solution. The journey to mastering knowledge management isn't about rigidly sticking to one tool but about exploring and finding the amalgamation that amplifies your capabilities the most.

Notion: The All-in-One Workspace
In the vast world of Personal Knowledge Management tools, Notion has carved out a unique space for itself, marrying functionality with elegance. Often heralded as a Swiss Army knife of digital productivity, Notion's appeal extends beyond just young professionals to a broader audience, all seeking an integrated solution for their digital workspace needs.

Features Overview:

Databases: Perhaps one of the most robust features of Notion, databases allow users to store and manipulate data in various formats, including tables, boards, calendars, and lists. Each entry in a database is a page, making it incredibly versatile for deep dives into individual items.

Pages: Within Notion, everything is a page. Whether you're drafting notes, creating a checklist, or even embedding another database, it all resides within pages. This hierarchical structure provides immense flexibility, allowing users to create nested pages, interlink them, or even link them to external resources.

Templates: To jump start workflows and reduce repetitive tasks, Notion comes equipped with a range of templates. From reading lists to travel planners, these templates can be used as-is or customized to individual needs. Moreover, the global community of Notion enthusiasts often shares their templates, broadening the available spectrum.

Integration's: Notion provides API access and integrates with popular tools like Slack, Google Calendar, and Trello. These integrations ensure that Notion can seamlessly fit into existing workflows, becoming a hub of activity and information.

Potential Use Cases:

Project Management: With its flexible database views, Notion can be set up as a kanban board, a timeline, or a list-based task manager. Combined with its collaborative features, this makes it ideal for team projects, keeping everyone on the same page—literally.

Note-taking: Beyond mere text, Notion's rich content options—like toggles, call outs, and embedded media—take note-taking to another level. Its linking feature allows users to create an interwoven web of notes, fostering a more connected knowledge base.

Knowledge Base Creation: Whether it's a personal wiki, a content calendar, or a digital garden, Notion's hierarchical page structure supports the development of expansive knowledge bases. These can be shared with others or kept private.

Strengths and Potential Drawbacks:

Strengths:

Versatility: Few tools match Notion's breadth of functionalities, all while maintaining a clean user interface.

Collaborative: With features like shared pages and real-time collaboration, Notion is perfect for team-based endeavors.
Extensive Community: Notion's user community is active and passionate, frequently sharing templates, tips, and workflows.

Potential Drawbacks:

Learning Curve: The very versatility that's a strength can also be daunting for newcomers. It may take time to understand and harness Notion's full potential.

Performance Issues: As a web-based platform, Notion can sometimes experience lag, especially with heavily populated pages or databases.
Offline Access: While Notion does offer offline capabilities, they're not as seamless or robust as some dedicated note-taking apps.

Notion, with its myriad of features, stands out as a premier choice for those looking to centralize their digital workspace. While it may require an initial investment of time to truly master, the potential rewards in terms of organization, efficiency, and collaboration are significant.

Roam Research: The Networked Thought Tool
Roam Research has been making waves in the Personal Knowledge Management (PKM) community for its unique approach to information organization. Touted as the tool for "networked thought," it takes a non-linear approach to note-taking, challenging traditional hierarchical systems and embracing the organic nature of human thought processes.

Features Overview:

Bi-directional Linking: Roams most distinctive feature, bi-directional linking, allows users to connect notes seamlessly. When you link to a page or create a new link, Roam automatically recognizes the connection, ensuring that thoughts and ideas are always interwoven and easily traceable.

Daily Notes: Every time you log into Roam, you're greeted with a blank page dated for the day. This encourages daily note-taking, reflection, and journaling. Over time, these daily entries form a rich tapestry of thoughts, ideas, and events.

Graph Views: This visual representation of your notes showcases how each entry is connected. It's not just a static diagram but an interactive map where you can see the nodes of ideas and their interconnections, providing a bird's eye view of your thought patterns and knowledge clusters.

Potential Use Cases:

Idea Interlinking: For writers, researchers, or thinkers who thrive on connecting disparate ideas, Roam offers a fluid platform to interlink thoughts and watch as they evolve and grow over time.

Zettelkasten Method Adaptation: The Zettelkasten method, a system of slip-box note-taking, finds a natural digital counterpart in Roam. The bi-directional linking aligns with Zettelkasten's emphasis on connecting notes, making knowledge retrieval and expansion more intuitive.

Journaling: Beyond professional use, many have adopted Roam for personal journaling. The daily notes feature fosters a habit of reflection, and the linking system helps trace personal growth, patterns, and insights over time.

Strengths and Potential Drawbacks:

Strengths:

Natural Thought Representation: Roams non-linear approach mirrors the way our minds work, jumping from one idea to another, seeing connections where there weren't any before.

Flexibility: There's no prescribed way to use Roam. It can be a structured knowledge base or a chaotic web of fleeting thoughts. It adapts to the user's style.

Community Ecosystem: Much like Notion, Roam has cultivated a passionate community that frequently shares use-cases, templates, and scripts to enhance functionality.

Potential Drawbacks:

Price Point: Roam Research comes with a subscription fee that's on the higher end compared to other PKM tools.

Initial Overwhelm: For those accustomed to traditional note-taking apps, Roams free-form structure can be disorienting initially.

Data Portability Concerns: Some users express concerns about the ease of exporting their data from Roam in a usable format, should they ever choose to migrate to a different platform.

In essence, Roam Research offers a fresh perspective on PKM, eschewing established norms and championing a more organic approach to information management. It may not be for everyone, but for those who click with its methodology, it's a revelation, opening up new avenues of thought exploration and knowledge synthesis.

Evernote: The Veteran Note-Taker

In the realm of Personal Knowledge Management (PKM) tools, Evernote stands tall as one of the pioneers, with over a decade of service to those eager to digitize, categorize, and synthesize their information. Its iconic elephant logo, symbolizing the intent to "never forget," aptly represents its mission: to be the trusted place for your life's work.

Features Overview:

Notebooks: Central to Evernote's structure, notebooks are digital binders where users can store and organize their notes. They can be stacked and categorized for more in-depth organization, enabling both broad and detailed categorization.

Tags: Beyond mere notebooks, tags offer another layer of categorization. A single note can have multiple tags, allowing for cross-referencing across different themes or topics.

Web Clipping: Evernote's web clipper is a beloved feature, permitting users to save articles, images, and pages directly from the web. This tool captures content in a clean format, storing it for offline viewing and tagging.

Search Capabilities: With Evernote's powerful search engine, no note remains hidden. Users can search for text within notes, images, PDFs, and even handwritten notes, ensuring that all captured information is easily retrievable.

Potential Use Cases:

Digital Filing Cabinet: Evernote can serve as a centralized repository for important documents, receipts, and personal records, making it a go-to tool for those eager to digitize and declutter their physical spaces.

Content Capture: Beyond traditional note-taking, Evernote excels at capturing varied forms of content—from web pages to images to audio notes. Journalists, writers, and researchers often use it as a digital net, catching fragments of information to be synthesized later.

Sharing: Whether it's sharing a shopping list with a partner or collaborating on a project, Evernote's note-sharing and collaboration features facilitate seamless digital teamwork.

Strengths and Potential Drawbacks:

Strengths:

Reliability: Having been around for a long time, Evernote boasts a proven track record of performance and data stability.

Cross-Platform Compatibility: Evernote shines in its availability across devices—from mobile to desktop to tablets, ensuring your notes are accessible anytime, anywhere.

Integration Ecosystem: With integration's spanning from Google Drive to Slack to Microsoft Teams, Evernote often fits seamlessly into existing digital workflows.

Potential Drawbacks:

Cost for Premium Features: While Evernote does offer a free version, many of its standout features, like offline access and more substantial upload limits, come at a premium cost.

Complexity for New Users: The depth of features can sometimes be daunting for newcomers, leading to a steeper learning curve.

Performance Hiccups: Some users report occasional slowdowns and sync issues, especially when handling larger notes or media-rich content.

Evernote, as a stalwart of the PKM world, remains relevant even as newer tools emerge. Its robust set of features, combined with its reliability, ensures that it remains a top choice for many. Whether used as a primary PKM tool or in conjunction with others, Evernote's versatility in capturing, organizing, and retrieving information makes it a cornerstone in the digital knowledge domain.

Spotlight on Other Prominent Tools

In the burgeoning world of Personal Knowledge Management (PKM), a plethora of tools exists, each with its unique set of features, capabilities, and loyal fan base. Beyond the giants like Notion, Roam Research, and Evernote, several other platforms have been making a significant impact in this domain. Let's shine a spotlight on some of them.

Obsidian: Local-first, linked knowledge base.
Obsidian is an up-and-coming player that emphasizes a local-first approach, meaning your notes reside on your device rather than a cloud. This appeals to users concerned about data privacy. Like Roam Research, Obsidian emphasizes linked thought with bi-directional links. Its graph view allows users to visualize their note connections, and its markdown-based system ensures easy formatting and export. For those who wish to keep their knowledge base offline yet interconnected, Obsidian offers a robust solution.

Trello: Visual project and knowledge management.
Though primarily known as a project management tool, Trello has been adopted by many as a PKM tool due to its visual and intuitive card-based system. Boards, lists, and cards can be used to organize knowledge, tasks, and projects. With integration like Butler, users can automate various workflows. Trello's flexibility allows it to be a digital whiteboard, a content calendar, a reading list, or a knowledge repository.

OneNote: Microsoft's versatile note-taking solution.
As part of the Microsoft Office suite, OneNote is a powerhouse in the note-taking arena. With a free form canvas-style approach, users can type, write, draw, or clip content from the web. Its hierarchical system of notebooks, sections, and pages allows for detailed organization. Integration with other Microsoft apps and a robust sync mechanism across devices makes it a top choice for those entrenched in the Microsoft ecosystem.

Anki: Spaced repetition for knowledge retention.
While most PKM tools focus on knowledge capture and organization, Anki specializes in retention. Utilizing the principle of spaced repetition, Anki

helps users memorize vast amounts of information, from languages to medical facts. Users create digital flashcards, and Anki schedules reviews based on how well the user remembers the content. This method ensures that knowledge is revisited just as it's about to be forgotten, cementing it more firmly in memory.

In the vast landscape of PKM tools, each platform has its strengths, philosophies, and areas of application. The modern knowledge worker is spoiled for choice, with a tool available for every need and preference. As the digital age progresses, it's heartening to see the evolution of tools that support, enhance, and elevate our pursuit of knowledge.

Comparing Tools: Which One is Right for You?

Navigating the vast seas of Personal Knowledge Management (PKM) tools can sometimes feel overwhelming. With each platform touting unique features and benefits, how does one choose? The answer lies not just in the tools themselves but also in introspecting about your needs, goals, and preferences.

Assessing Individual Needs:

Purpose: Start by defining your primary goal. Are you looking for a digital journaling space, a research tool, a project manager, or perhaps a comprehensive knowledge repository? Some tools excel in specific areas while offering baseline functionality in others.

Volume of Information: If you're managing a few notes or daily to-dos, your needs might be different from someone archiving years of research. Certain tools handle vast volumes better, providing faster search and categorization features.

Collaboration Requirements: Solo users might prioritize different features compared to teams. If you're hoping to collaborate, look for tools with robust sharing, commenting, and real-time editing capabilities.

Personal Workflow: Your unique way of processing and organizing information matters. Do you prefer a linear, hierarchical structure or a more free-form, interconnected web of ideas? Your comfort with the tool's layout and functionality will significantly impact your productivity.

Customization vs. Out-of-the-Box Functionality:

Some users value the ability to customize every aspect of their PKM space, tailoring it to their whims and needs. Platforms like Notion or Obsidian cater to this, offering immense flexibility. However, this customization might come at the cost of a steeper learning curve.

On the other hand, if you want a tool that's intuitive from the get-go, with less tinkering required, options like Evernote or OneNote might be more up your alley. They offer robust out-of-the-box functionality that requires minimal setup.

Short-term and Long-term Considerations:

Portability: Think about the future. You might change devices, platforms, or even the tools themselves. Ensuring that the tool you choose has reliable export features means you can take your data with you, no matter where you go.

Backup: Digital tools, while immensely powerful, aren't infallible. Opt for platforms that offer automated backups, cloud sync, or easy manual backup procedures.

Scaling: Your knowledge base will grow, and so will your needs. A tool that's perfect for a handful of notes might become cumbersome with thousands. Consider how the tool handles scaling, both in terms of volume and complexity.

Choosing the right PKM tool is a deeply personal endeavor. It's a blend of the tool's capabilities and how they align with your goals, preferences, and future plans. Investing time in understanding these aspects ensures you'll pick a platform that not only stores your knowledge but truly augments it.

Integrating Multiple Tools for a Holistic PKM System

The rich ecosystem of PKM tools offers an array of possibilities. For many, a single tool doesn't encapsulate all their knowledge management needs. Instead, they find value in harnessing the strengths of multiple platforms. However, integrating various tools into a cohesive system requires careful planning and strategy.

Syncing and Cross-Referencing Between Tools:

In the digital age, the ability to interlink tools is invaluable. Integrations can transform disjointed platforms into a unified powerhouse of knowledge management.

APIs and Plugins: Many advanced PKM tools, like Notion or Trello, offer APIs (Application Programming Interfaces) or support third-party plugins. This allows them to interact with other software, pulling or pushing data as required.

Zapier and IFTTT: Platforms like Zapier or IFTTT act as bridges between different tools. For instance, a note taken on Evernote can be automatically mirrored in Notion or a task created in Trello can reflect in Todoist.

Manual Cross-Referencing: Even in the absence of direct integrations, one can establish a manual system of cross-referencing. Using unique IDs, tags, or consistent naming conventions can help trace a piece of knowledge across tools.

Avoiding Over-Complication: The Balance Between Tool Diversity and Simplicity.

While integrating tools can amplify your PKM system's capabilities, there's a risk of creating a complex web that's hard to navigate and maintain.

Purpose-Driven Tool Selection: Before incorporating a new tool, clearly define its purpose. If Tool A is for task management and Tool B for long-form note-taking, resist the temptation to let their functions overlap excessively.

Centralized Hub: Designate one tool as your primary or central hub, a space where the majority of your activities begin or end. It can act as the gateway to other specialized tools, ensuring you have a clear starting point.

Regular Audits: Periodically review your system. If you find certain tools are redundant or underutilized, it might be time to phase them out or consolidate.

Embrace Simplicity: A complex system isn't necessarily an efficient one. If integrating another tool adds marginal value but considerable complexity, it might be worth reconsidering. Remember, the aim is to enhance productivity, not hinder it.

In the pursuit of the perfect PKM system, the allure of adding "just one more tool" can be tempting. However, the true power lies in crafting a seamless, intuitive, and efficient workflow. By thoughtfully integrating tools and regularly reassessing their utility, you can construct a holistic PKM system that truly serves your knowledge management needs.

As we journey through the vast terrain of Personal Knowledge Management (PKM) and delve into the myriad of tools at our disposal, it's essential to remember the larger picture.

Tools as Enablers, Not Solutions in Themselves:

While the digital age presents us with a multitude of advanced platforms and intricate functionalities, it's crucial to recognize that these tools are merely instruments. They are designed to facilitate, augment, and enhance our knowledge management processes. Yet, they cannot replace the intellectual rigor, curiosity, and discernment that each individual brings to the table. A tool, no matter how sophisticated, can't replace human intuition or the value of organic thought processes. Instead, they are there to assist, streamline, and amplify.

Experimentation and Evolution:

The realm of PKM isn't static. As we grow, both personally and professionally, our needs shift, our goals evolve, and our approach to managing knowledge transforms. Likewise, the technological landscape is in a state of perpetual motion, with new tools emerging and existing ones constantly upgrading.

In this dynamic setting:

Be Open to Experimentation: Just as a chef might try various utensils before finding the perfect knife, it's entirely reasonable for knowledge professionals to test multiple tools before settling on what works best for them.

Revisit and Revise: What serves you today might not be as effective tomorrow. Regularly review your toolkit, making adjustments as necessary. It ensures that your system remains aligned with your objectives and stays resilient against changing demands.

Stay Informed: As new technologies emerge, take the time to explore and understand them. Even if you don't adopt every new tool, being aware of the possibilities can inspire innovative approaches to your PKM practices.

Trust Yourself: While it's beneficial to learn from others' systems and strategies, remember that your unique perspective, needs, and experiences will shape your PKM journey. Trust in your insights and be patient with your process.

Mastering knowledge in the digital age is both an art and a science. While tools play a pivotal role, it's the human spirit of inquiry, adaptability, and lifelong learning that truly drives knowledge forward. Embrace the tools, but more importantly, celebrate the intellectual voyage they support. Remember, it's not about the destination but the enriching journey of continuous discovery and growth.

Chapter 5:

Building Your Personal Knowledge System

Crafting a System Tailored to You

In today's fast-paced digital age, information is abundant, but true knowledge is a craft. For young professionals navigating a complex, ever-evolving professional landscape, harnessing this craft can make the difference between thriving and merely surviving. Thus, developing a Personal Knowledge Management (PKM) system is not only invaluable but also imperative. The essence of this chapter is to underline the significance of crafting a PKM system that mirrors your unique aspirations, learning style, and professional demands.

The Importance of a Systematic Approach to PKM

Imagine wading through a dense forest without a map or compass. The sheer volume of trees, the underbrush, the diverse paths – it's overwhelming. This forest is akin to the digital knowledge space we navigate daily. Just like in the forest, where having the right tools – a map, a compass, perhaps even a guide – makes the journey manageable and productive, a systematic approach to PKM equips you to extract relevance from the vastness of available information.

Being systematic doesn't mean being rigid. On the contrary, it is about having a structured framework that can flexibly adapt to new learning, challenges, and changes. A well-honed PKM system streamlines your efforts, preventing you from getting mired in information overload. It helps to transform raw information into actionable insights, amplifying your professional efficacy and agility.

Moving Beyond Tools: The Synergy of Methodology and Technology

When considering PKM, the immediate thought for many is technology. We live in an era graced by tools for every conceivable task: apps for note-taking, platforms for collaboration, software for organizing, and algorithms for filtering. But to regard PKM as just a collection of digital tools is to miss the forest for the trees.

At its core, PKM is the synergy of methodology and technology. While tools play a role, they are merely instruments, waiting for the musician to give them life. The methodology you choose, the strategies you employ, and the habits you cultivate are the real bedrock of effective PKM. Together, methodology and technology create a resonating synergy, allowing you to not just manage but master knowledge.

In essence, as you journey through this chapter, you will discover that building your personal knowledge system is not about accumulating tools but about refining a mindset. It is a deliberate quest to curate, assimilate, and apply knowledge, utilizing tools as aides but relying foremost on your tailored methodology.

As we delve deeper into crafting your personalized PKM system, remember this: The digital age is not about who has the most information, but who can harness it most effectively. Your PKM system, tailored to your unique needs and aspirations, will be your compass and map, guiding you through the dense forests of the digital knowledge world.

Laying the Foundation: Setting Clear Objectives

In the realm of construction, the strength and durability of a building rest upon the foundation it's built upon. Analogously, as we embark on the journey of crafting a robust Personal Knowledge Management system, it's of utmost importance to lay a foundation grounded in distinct objectives. Such objectives serve as the compass, illuminating the path of your knowledge management pursuits.

Understanding your motivations is the starting line. Why do you need a PKM system? This isn't a rhetorical question; it demands genuine contemplation. For many, the drive might be career advancement. In the ever-evolving professional landscape, being abreast of the latest technologies, methodologies, and practices offers a competitive advantage. For others, the PKM system might be a vessel for lifelong learning. The world is an expansive reservoir of knowledge, with realms ranging from the nuances of a new language, the intricacies of historical events, to the enigmas of quantum physics. Then there are those who view PKM as the linchpin in effective project management. With multiple resources, timelines, research, and stakeholders to juggle, PKM becomes an invaluable asset in ensuring smooth execution.

Amidst this, it's pivotal to discern between three terms that often become intertwined in the PKM discourse: tool, method, and system.

A tool can be visualized as a tangible instrument or application tailored to aid in a specific task. If we were to draw a parallel to cooking, tools are akin to the utensils gracing a kitchen - be it the sharp knife, the versatile spatula, or the whirling whisk. Translating this to the PKM universe, tools manifest as software applications; Evernote serving as a canvas for note-taking or Trello morphing into an aide for task management.

In contrast, a method is the strategy or structured approach one adopts to realize a desired outcome. Drawing from our cooking analogy, if tools were the utensils, the method is the recipe. It's the sequence, the steps, the dance of ingredients. In the world of PKM, methods take the form of techniques; some might find solace in the Feynman Technique to delve deeper into topics, while others might embrace the Pomodoro Technique to manage time proficiently.

Then we arrive at the system, which emerges as the grand orchestration of tools and methods. It's the symphony where each tool and method plays its part, harmonizing to fulfill a broader objective. In our culinary narrative, the system is the entire meal preparation process, where utensils and recipes synchronize to create a delightful dish.

In essence, as you sculpt your PKM foundation, let your objectives be the guiding force, and always remain cognizant of the distinctions and interplay's between tools, methods, and systems. They are the trinity that will elevate your knowledge management from mere information collection to mastery.

Steps to Set Up a PKM System

Embarking on the journey of establishing a PKM system is akin to constructing a bridge. Just as a bridge connects two shores, a PKM system bridges the chasm between abundant information and actionable knowledge. And like any engineering feat, setting up a PKM system requires a methodical approach.

Assessment: Evaluating Current Knowledge Management Habits and Pinpointing Gaps

Before laying the first brick or drawing the first line, it's essential to assess the terrain. Begin by introspecting on your existing habits of knowledge management. Are you an avid note-taker? Do you often find digital articles to read later? Are you frequently overwhelmed by the sheer volume of information? Evaluating your current practices gives you a clear picture of where you stand. By identifying gaps, you also get a sense of the bridges you need to build to transition from your current state to your desired PKM system.

Selection: Choosing the Appropriate Tools and Platforms Based on Individual Needs

Once you have a firm grasp of your current position and the gaps you need to bridge, the next phase involves selecting your tools and platforms. Remember, there isn't a one-size-fits-all solution. While some might find solace in digital platforms, others might lean towards analog systems, and some may thrive in a hybrid space. The crux is to choose tools that align with your personal needs, learning style, and objectives.

Structuring: Setting Up Templates, Folders, Tags, and Initial Categorization

With the tools in place, it's time to give shape to your PKM system. Think of it as the architecture and design phase. Set up templates that guide your note-taking. Create folders to segregate different types of knowledge. Employ tags to quickly locate and interlink related pieces of information. The initial categorization serves as the backbone of your PKM, allowing for smooth navigation in the future.

Habit Formation: Designing Routines for Regular Knowledge Input, Review, and Application

A bridge, no matter how elegantly designed, is futile if not traversed. Similarly, a PKM system, irrespective of its sophistication, is redundant without regular use. Cultivating habits is the key. Carve out dedicated time slots for knowledge input, be it reading articles, watching tutorials, or attending webinars. Set aside periodic intervals for reviewing and consolidating what you've learned. And most importantly, find avenues to apply your acquired knowledge, for it is in application that true mastery is born.

Iteration and Evolution: Periodically Revisiting and Tweaking the System for Optimization

Finally, understand that your PKM system is not set in stone. As you grow, evolve, and encounter new challenges, your system should mirror that dynamism. Periodically revisit your PKM architecture. Reflect on what's working and what's not. Tweak and iterate based on your reflections. A PKM system, at its best, is an evolving entity, consistently optimized for the ever-changing landscapes of the digital age.

Strategies for Consistent Knowledge Capture

In the vast ocean of information that constitutes the digital realm, knowledge capture can be likened to casting a net. But it's not just about casting it anywhere—it's about casting it wisely and consistently to ensure a fruitful catch every time. This section delves into effective strategies to cultivate a consistent rhythm of knowledge capture, ensuring that not a single valuable piece of information slips through.

Setting Aside Dedicated 'Capture' Times: Daily or Weekly Reviews

Much like how a fisherman allocates specific hours of the day when fish are most active, dedicating specific times for knowledge capture can exponentially enhance its efficacy. Whether you prefer daily short bursts of review or a comprehensive weekly reflection, the regularity ensures that you stay updated. These dedicated times become sanctuaries of learning, allowing you to assimilate, categorize, and reflect upon the information you've garnered. By making it a ritual, it soon transforms into second nature, ensuring consistent and effective knowledge capture.

Using Mobile Tools and Widgets for On-the-Go Capture

The digital age we live in is characterized by mobility. As life's pace accelerates, waiting to capture knowledge until you're seated at your desk might lead to missed opportunities. Mobile tools and widgets come to the rescue here. They serve as your digital fishing rod, always at the ready. Whether you've just stumbled upon a profound article while commuting or attended an enlightening webinar during lunch, mobile tools ensure that insights are captured then and there, without delay.

The Role of Triggers: Setting Reminders and Using Prompts to Facilitate Knowledge Input

Even the most seasoned fisherman sometimes needs a reminder—perhaps about a change in weather or tides. Similarly, in the bustling routine of professional life, it's easy to overlook knowledge capture. This is where triggers play a crucial role. Setting reminders on your devices or even sticking post-it notes at your workstation can serve as gentle nudges. Furthermore, prompts can be instrumental in facilitating deeper reflection. A prompt might be a question like "What did I learn today?" or "How can this knowledge be applied in my current project?" By engaging with these prompts, the process of knowledge capture becomes more ingrained, methodical, and reflexive.

A well-honed strategy for consistent knowledge capture is the linchpin of a robust PKM system. By allocating dedicated times, leveraging the power of mobile tools, and harnessing the potency of triggers, you ensure that the vast seas of information consistently yield valuable insights, enriching your personal and professional journey.

Organizing Information for Optimal Flow

Imagine the intricate choreography of a ballet performance. Dancers seamlessly weave through each other, following a meticulous arrangement to ensure the audience captures every movement, every emotion. Similarly, in the world of Personal Knowledge Management, organizing information is akin to this choreography. To derive value from captured knowledge, it's crucial that it flows seamlessly, is easily retrievable, and above all, actionable. Here, we explore strategies to ensure your knowledge dances with grace and purpose.

Hierarchical vs. Networked Organization: When to Use Which

The age-old debate of hierarchical versus networked organization mirrors the classic dichotomy of tree versus web. In a hierarchical setup, knowledge is compartmentalized into distinct categories and sub-categories, reminiscent of a tree's trunk branching out into limbs and twigs. It's ideal for topics that have clear boundaries and for users who think in structured, compartmentalized manners.

Conversely, a networked organization is like a web, where pieces of knowledge interlink based on relationships, themes, or insights. It thrives in environments where boundaries blur, and interconnectedness is key. While the hierarchical approach can help in quickly narrowing down to a specific sub-topic, the networked approach shines in drawing unexpected connections between seemingly unrelated pieces of information.

Your choice between the two hinges on the nature of the information at hand and your cognitive style. Often, a fusion of both can offer a rich, multi-dimensional perspective.

The Power of Tagging: Facilitating Cross-Referenced and Thematic Searches

Tagging is to knowledge what spices are to a dish – it enhances, categorizes, and adds depth. By attaching relevant tags to pieces of information, you introduce a layer of categorization that transcends the confines of folders or directories. Whether you're searching for all content related to a particular theme, drawing parallels between different projects, or looking for patterns, tags serve as powerful anchors. They make cross-referenced searches a breeze, and thematic dives deep and meaningful.

Creating Index or Dashboard Pages: A Central Hub for Key Resources and Ongoing Projects

In the bustling city scape of knowledge, an index or dashboard page acts as the town square, a nexus where pivotal paths converge. By creating such central hubs, you have at your fingertips a snapshot of your key resources and ongoing projects. Think of it as your command center, where you can swiftly navigate to various sectors of your knowledge base, monitor progress, and identify areas that require attention. An effectively designed dashboard reduces the cognitive load, ensuring that you spend less time searching and more time learning and implementing.

In the grand ballet of knowledge, organizing information for optimal flow ensures that each piece, each insight, each nugget of wisdom is choreographed to perfection. When knowledge flows with ease, it becomes not just a passive repository but an active, dynamic force propelling personal and professional growth.

Categorizing for Easy Retrieval

Navigating the vast landscape of knowledge without a clear categorization is akin to traversing a dense forest without a map. While the journey might be adventurous, it could also be time-consuming, overwhelming, and less productive. Categorization serves as this map, making it not only easy to place knowledge accurately but also retrieve it efficiently. Let's delve into the art and science of categorizing knowledge for easy retrieval.

Establishing Broad Categories Based on Domains or Disciplines

Starting with broad categories is the first step in making sense of a sea of information. Think of these as the primary compass directions guiding your journey. Based on the nature of your profession or interests, these categories could be established around domains or disciplines such as "Technology", "Design", "Marketing", or "Literature". By having these primary bins, you ensure that every piece of information you come across has a preliminary home, a broad tent under which it can find shelter.

Sub-categorization Strategies: Project-based, Time-based, or Theme-based

Diving deeper into the categorization forest requires you to carve out pathways, ensuring you can reach the exact location of a piece of knowledge. Sub-categorization is that process. Depending on your unique needs and the nature of the information, you can adopt various strategies:

Project-based: Ideal for professionals working on multiple projects simultaneously. This strategy enables you to segregate information based on individual projects, making retrieval straightforward.

Time-based: If your work or learning is more chronological, categorizing based on time frames, be it years, months, or even specific events, might be beneficial. Researchers or historians might find this especially valuable.

Theme-based: For those who engage in thematic or interdisciplinary work, this is a potent strategy. It allows knowledge to be grouped based on overarching themes, making connections and interdisciplinary exploration smoother.

The Dynamic Nature of Categorization: Merging, Splitting, and Evolving Categories Over Time

Like the forest, which evolves over seasons, your knowledge landscape is not static. It's dynamic, growing, and shifting. Hence, your categorization strategy should mirror this dynamism. As you gather more insights, some categories might become too vast, necessitating a split. Conversely, some categories might be too narrow, making merging a logical step. Over time, new disciplines or interests might emerge, and old ones might fade, leading to the birth or retirement of categories. Embracing this fluidity ensures your categorization remains relevant, efficient, and in tune with your evolving knowledge needs.

In conclusion, a well-structured categorization strategy is the backbone of an effective PKM system. By ensuring that every piece of information is mapped accurately and is easily retrievable, you transform your knowledge base from a dense, intimidating forest into a well-marked, welcoming sanctuary of insights and wisdom.

Streamlining and Maintenance

A flourishing garden, no matter how beautifully planned and initially set up, requires regular maintenance to keep it at its best. Overgrown shrubs need pruning, fallen leaves need sweeping, and sometimes, plants need replanting. Similarly, a Personal Knowledge Management system, irrespective of its initial organization, requires constant streamlining and maintenance to ensure it remains relevant, accessible, and efficient. This section will guide you through the practices that keep your PKM garden thriving.

The Importance of Periodic System Clean-Ups

Just as leaves and debris accumulate in a garden, in a PKM system, outdated information, redundant files, or even stray notes that lack context can accumulate over time. If left unchecked, this clutter can make navigation cumbersome and reduce the system's overall efficiency. By committing to periodic system clean-ups, be it monthly, quarterly, or annually, you ensure that your system remains streamlined. This not only helps in quick retrieval of pertinent information but also reduces the cognitive load when interacting with the system.

Archiving vs. Deleting: Keeping Your System Clutter-Free While Preserving Essential Knowledge

When tending to a garden, the gardener is faced with decisions: which plants to prune, which to transplant, and which to remove entirely.

Similarly, when streamlining your PKM system, it's crucial to discern between what to archive and what to delete.

Archiving is akin to transplanting—it's about preserving information that might not be immediately relevant but holds value for future reference. It ensures that your main workspace remains clutter-free while still having access to archived knowledge when required.

Deleting, on the other hand, is about removing what's truly redundant or irrelevant, much like uprooting a plant that's no longer thriving. It's essential to approach this step with caution, ensuring you're not discarding something that might hold latent value.

Backup and Security: Ensuring Your Knowledge Base Remains Intact and Confidential

A garden is exposed to external threats, be it pests, weather extremities, or potential trespassers. Similarly, a PKM system, especially in the digital realm, is susceptible to data loss, hardware failures, or even unauthorized access. Hence, just as a gardener would install a fence or use protective measures, it's paramount to ensure the security and backup of your PKM system.

Regularly backing up your system ensures that, in the event of unforeseen circumstances, your carefully curated knowledge remains safe. On the other hand, employing security measures, be it strong passwords, encryption, or two-factor authentication, guarantees the confidentiality and integrity of your knowledge base.

In essence, the journey of mastering knowledge in the digital age doesn't end once a PKM system is set up. Much like a garden, it requires continuous care, attention, and sometimes even reinvention. By committing to regular streamlining and maintenance, you ensure that your PKM system remains a flourishing haven of insights, evolving alongside you.

Troubleshooting Common Challenges

Like any endeavor of value and complexity, managing a Personal Knowledge Management system isn't devoid of its challenges. Imagine setting out on a grand voyage across seas; while the ship, the map, and the compass are all in place, unpredictable storms, elusive winds, or even moments of self-doubt can interrupt the journey. In the course of mastering PKM, certain challenges might rear their heads. Fear not, for this section will equip you with the navigational expertise to steer through these rough seas with finesse.

Overcoming Resistance to Regular Knowledge Input

Every seasoned sailor knows that sometimes the winds just don't blow in your favor. Similarly, there might be days or even phases when the resistance to regular knowledge input feels palpable. It could stem from mental fatigue, an overwhelming influx of information, or even doubts about the utility of what's being documented.

To combat this, reconnect with your 'why'. Remind yourself of the objectives that prompted your PKM journey. Sometimes, a brief hiatus, giving yourself permission to pause, can reignite the passion for learning. Alternatively, establishing simple rituals, like a fixed time for daily knowledge input or coupling it with a pleasant activity, can transform it from a daunting task to a cherished routine.

Addressing Tool Overwhelm: Sticking to Essentials and Avoiding Shiny Object Syndrome

The seas of the digital age are dotted with an array of tools, each promising to be the next game-changer for your PKM system. While it's tempting to hoist every tool aboard, this can lead to tool overwhelm. The allure of new features, interfaces, or functionalities—often termed as the 'shiny object syndrome'—can scatter focus and dilute the effectiveness of your system.

The antidote? Start by identifying the essential functions you need in your PKM toolkit. Before incorporating a new tool, evaluate its alignment with your objectives and its utility in simplifying your processes. Remember, sometimes less is more. A few tools mastered profoundly can often yield better results than a plethora of them used superficially.

Navigating the Balance Between Structure and Flexibility

Charting a voyage requires a clear map and structure. However, sticking rigidly to it, even when the seas change, can lead to missed opportunities or challenges. The same holds for a PKM system. While structure is pivotal for organizing and retrieving knowledge, excessive rigidity can stifle growth, creativity, and the assimilation of evolving insights.

To navigate this delicate balance, regularly revisit and reassess your system's structure. Is it facilitating your goals, or has it become a restrictive mold? Being open to iteration, allowing your system to breathe and grow organically, can usher in a harmonious blend of structure and flexibility.

The journey of PKM, much like a sea voyage, is as much about the challenges faced as it is about the destinations reached. By preemptively recognizing these challenges and equipping oneself with strategies to troubleshoot them, you ensure that your PKM ship sails smoothly, harnessing the winds of the digital age to propel towards mastery.

As we draw the curtains on this chapter about constructing and nurturing a robust Personal Knowledge Management system, it's imperative to take a moment to reflect on the journey itself. Building a personal knowledge system isn't an endeavor that one accomplishes overnight and then sets aside. It's not a static monument, but rather a flowing river, with its ebbs, flows, tributaries, and occasional meanders.

Reflecting on the Ongoing Nature of Personal Knowledge System Building

The digital age is characterized by its rapid pace and the incessant evolution of knowledge. As such, the task of knowledge system building is perpetual. Just as a river continually receives water from its tributaries, your PKM system will consistently be fed with new information, insights, and experiences. This ongoing nature can be both exhilarating and demanding. It's a commitment to lifelong learning, an acknowledgment that as the world advances, so must our methods of capturing, organizing, and applying knowledge.

Encouraging Readers to Remain Adaptable

With the constantly changing landscape of the digital age, adaptability becomes a crucial trait. Your PKM system, as structured and organized as it may be, shouldn't become rigid. Imagine it as a tree. While its roots are firmly grounded, signifying the foundational principles and objectives of your knowledge journey, its branches must be flexible, swaying and adjusting to the winds of change.

Recognizing that your PKM system is a living entity is pivotal. Just as a tree grows, shedding old leaves and sprouting new branches, your system will evolve. There might be tools and techniques that become obsolete, and there will be novel approaches that emerge. Being receptive to this change, actively seeking refinements, and periodically pruning and reshaping your system ensures it remains vibrant, relevant, and effective.

To conclude, mastering knowledge in the digital age is a journey, not a destination. It demands dedication, agility, and a recognition of the symbiotic relationship between the learner and the system. As you embark or continue on this voyage, remember to cherish the process, remain adaptable, and above all, revel in the joy of learning, organizing, and applying knowledge in this ever-evolving digital epoch.

Chapter 6:
Curating and Filtering Information

The Art and Science of Curation

In the vast expanse of the digital cosmos, there exists an ever-expanding universe of information. Each day, this universe witnesses the birth of countless new stars—articles, podcasts, videos, tweets, and more. Amidst this dazzling and sometimes overwhelming celestial display, how does one pinpoint those stars which illuminate our path the brightest? This is where the art and science of curation come into play.

Navigating the Digital Information Deluge

Today's digital age has democratized the creation and dissemination of information to an unprecedented degree. This democratization, while a beacon of progress, has also resulted in an avalanche of content, a deluge that can sometimes drown even the most voracious of knowledge seekers.

However, as challenging as this downpour may seem, it's essential to view it as a bountiful rain, nurturing the soil of our intellect. The key is in developing the skill to channel this rain, ensuring it nourishes us without overwhelming. This channeling, or more aptly, curating, allows us to extract value, derive insights, and construct meaningful narratives from the ocean of information available at our fingertips.

The Increasing Importance of Discernment in a Saturated Knowledge Landscape

In an age where quantity often overshadows quality, discernment emerges as a pivotal skill. Curating isn't just about gathering; it's about gathering judiciously. It's akin to a jeweler meticulously selecting gems for a necklace, ensuring each one adds value and complements the other.

This discernment is no longer a luxury but a necessity. In a landscape saturated with knowledge of varying credibility and relevance, the ability to differentiate wheat from chaff becomes paramount. As we delve deeper into this chapter, we'll explore the tools, techniques, and mindsets that can transform you into an adept curator, enabling you to navigate the digital seas with precision, purpose, and panache.

Recognizing Quality and Relevance

Navigating the vast expanse of digital knowledge is akin to a treasure hunt, where each seeker aims to discover the most valuable gems hidden amidst the overwhelming clutter. Recognizing the true value of these gems is an art and a skill that demands a keen sense of judgment.

One of the primary considerations when evaluating the worth of a piece of information is its source credibility. Trustworthiness is often derived from the reputation of its origin, be it a renowned institution, an industry expert, or a credible publication. Reliable sources form the bedrock on which solid knowledge structures are built.

Yet, as essential as the source is, timeliness plays a crucial role as well. In an era characterized by its fast-paced nature, some information gains value by virtue of its immediacy. Conversely, certain knowledge stands resilient against the test of time, never losing its relevance or worth.

In addition to these, the direct applicability of information often decides its place in one's curated collection. Pieces of knowledge that align seamlessly with one's current projects, objectives, or areas of interest usually hold more weight. Such resonance ensures that the acquired knowledge doesn't just sit idle but is actively applied and utilized.

Lastly, the depth of the content can't be overlooked. The richness of a meticulously researched study or a thoroughly analyzed article offers insights that a cursory glance or a surface-level piece might overlook. However, it's equally essential to understand the balance between breadth and depth. While diving deep provides a comprehensive understanding of a particular subject, skimming across various topics ensures a broader perspective. The true art of curation lies in knowing when to hover on the surface and when to plunge into the depths.

To illustrate this balance and the criteria of selection more vividly, one can look at case studies that compare the lifespan and impact of fleeting trends against evergreen knowledge. Such comparisons often spotlight the transient nature of certain popular content while underscoring the lasting value of foundational information.

In essence, the journey of curating is less about amassing vast quantities of information and more about discerning the quality and relevance of what one chooses to incorporate into their knowledge arsenal.

Techniques to Determine the Relevance and Value of Information

In the quest for curating a robust knowledge base, having a set of reliable techniques to evaluate information becomes indispensable. These methods provide a structured approach, allowing curators to sift through content efficiently, ensuring only the most relevant and valuable pieces make the cut.

The time-tested approach of The Five W's is often a good starting point. By asking *Who* produced the information, *What* the central theme or message is, *When* it was created or updated, *Where* it was sourced from, and *Why* it may be significant or relevant, one can gain a comprehensive understanding of the content. These questions act as a sieve, filtering out irrelevant details and homing in on the crux.

Another effective method is Cross-referencing. This involves juxtaposing new information against one's existing knowledge or comparing it with other sources. By doing so, inconsistencies can be spotted, and the reliability of the information can be assessed. Furthermore, cross-referencing helps in placing new knowledge in the context of what one already knows, enriching the overall understanding and creating a cohesive knowledge network.

Then there's the Feynman Technique, named after the renowned physicist Richard Feynman. This technique is rooted in the idea of breaking down complex concepts into simple terms, as if explaining to a child. By attempting to simplify a piece of information or a concept to its bare essentials, one can gauge their understanding. If the simplification is challenging, it might indicate gaps in comprehension or the potential irrelevance of the information. Conversely, if a topic can be distilled easily, it often signifies a solid grasp and the relevance of that knowledge.

By incorporating these techniques into the curation process, one ensures a more rigorous and methodical approach to knowledge acquisition. This not only enhances the quality of the curated content but also reinforces one's understanding and appreciation of the chosen material.

Filtering Mechanisms: Tools and Methods

The act of curation, while being discerning, often requires assistance, especially when faced with the continuous influx of digital information. This is where filtering mechanisms—both technological and human-driven —play a pivotal role, acting as sentinels that ensure only the most relevant and valuable content makes its way to the curator.

Automated Tools

The digital age offers a plethora of tools designed to streamline the curation process. Among them, RSS feed filters stand out, allowing users to subscribe to specific content sources and receive updates in real-time. By setting precise criteria or topics of interest, one can ensure that they're always abreast of the latest and most relevant publications in their domain.

Equally valuable are keyword alerts. Services like Google Alerts enable individuals to receive notifications whenever their predefined terms or phrases appear online. This is especially useful for staying updated on niche topics, emerging trends, or specific areas of interest.

Moreover, with advancements in artificial intelligence, AI-driven content recommendations have emerged as a formidable ally in the curation journey. These algorithms analyze user preferences, browsing habits, and interactions to suggest articles, studies, and content pieces tailored to individual tastes and requirements. Such personalisation ensures that the curator spends less time sifting through irrelevant material and more time diving deep into pertinent content.

Personal Content Audits

Despite the efficacy of automated tools, the human touch remains irreplaceable. Personal content audits involve periodically revisiting the sources of information one relies on. This self-reflective process enables the curator to assess the ongoing relevance of these sources, prune outdated or less valuable ones, and add fresh, emerging platforms that offer richer insights.

Community and Expert Recommendations

No individual, no matter how dedicated, can scour the entirety of the digital realm. This is where the power of community and expert recommendations shines. Leveraging collective wisdom means tapping into the insights and findings of fellow knowledge seekers, industry experts, and thought leaders. By doing so, one can discover high-quality content that might have otherwise slipped through the cracks.

In essence, filtering mechanisms serve as the gatekeepers of quality in the curation process. They ensure that each piece of content, whether discovered through automated tools, personal audits, or community recommendations, aligns with the curator's standards of relevance and value.

Avoiding the Pitfalls of Confirmation Bias

In the expansive world of digital information, while the quest for relevance and quality remains paramount, another lurking challenge often goes overlooked: confirmation bias. This cognitive blind spot, deeply ingrained in human psychology, subtly influences our choices and preferences, potentially skewing our knowledge base and perspective.

Understanding the Psychology of Confirmation Bias

At its core, confirmation bias represents our innate tendency to favor information that aligns with our pre-existing beliefs while often dismissing or overlooking contradictory data. This is not merely a matter of preference; it's a deep-seated cognitive function aimed at preserving our mental models and worldviews. Over time, if unchecked, this bias can lead to an echo chamber effect, where our curated knowledge becomes one-dimensional and lacks the richness of varied perspectives.

Strategies to Actively Seek Diverse Perspectives

Combating confirmation bias requires intentional effort. One effective strategy involves actively seeking out opposing viewpoints and alternative perspectives. By deliberately engaging with content that challenges our beliefs, we not only broaden our horizons but also strengthen our understanding of the subjects at hand. Such engagement can be as simple as following thought leaders with different viewpoints or participating in forums that encourage constructive debates.

Additionally, practicing self-reflection plays a significant role. Periodically questioning the basis of our beliefs, and the sources from which they originate, helps in identifying potential biases and rectifying them.

The Importance of Varied Information Sources

Diversifying the pool of information sources is a tangible way to minimize the effects of confirmation bias. Consuming content beyond one's comfort zone or typical spheres of interest ensures exposure to a broader range of ideas, opinions, and facts. This can mean delving into publications from different cultures, exploring interdisciplinary journals, or even listening to podcasts that discuss unconventional viewpoints.

For instance, a tech professional might benefit from reading sociological studies, providing a different lens through which to view technological advancements. Or a staunch proponent of a particular economic theory could engage with material supporting an opposing school of thought, thereby refining their understanding and arguments.

While the digital age offers unprecedented access to knowledge, it also poses challenges that require vigilance and intentionality. Avoiding the pitfalls of confirmation bias ensures that our curated knowledge remains rich, diverse, and reflective of the multifaceted world we inhabit.

Critical Thinking: The Heart of Effective Curation

Navigating the vast digital seascape, curators are often at risk of being engulfed by waves of information. The anchor that keeps them grounded is the ability to think critically. Rather than simply accepting information at face value, effective curation demands a rigorous examination of content for its quality and relevance. This discernment is rooted deeply in the principles of critical thinking.

At the very essence of critical thinking lies the component of Analysis. This process involves dissecting complex information or concepts to understand their underlying structure and nuances. By segmenting information into its fundamental elements, curators gain clarity, ensuring that they're not misled by superficial or misrepresented details.

Then comes the phase of Evaluation, where curators judge the credibility, relevance, and overall value of information. In this stage, discerning objective facts from personal opinions becomes paramount. The ability to differentiate between genuine insights and inherent biases ensures that the curated knowledge stands on a solid foundation of truth.

On this foundation, curators employ Inference to draw meaningful conclusions. This skill requires recognizing patterns, connecting disparate pieces of information, and making educated predictions. Inference is the bridge between passive information consumption and active knowledge application.

Lastly, amidst the whirlwind of curation, taking a step back to engage in Reflection becomes essential. Through this introspective process, curators assess the validity of their beliefs, decisions, and actions. By regularly revisiting and reassessing their knowledge base, they ensure its continued relevance and accuracy.

Yet, while skepticism is a trusted ally in the curation process, there's a fine line that separates it from cynicism. Encouraging skepticism means fostering an attitude of open-minded questioning. It's about probing, verifying, and being cautious without dismissing information outright. On the other hand, cynicism can lead to a rigid mindset, closing doors to potential insights.

To cultivate and sharpen the sword of critical thinking, incorporating practical exercises into one's daily routine can prove invaluable. For instance, challenging oneself to debate both sides of an argument, discussing topics with individuals holding opposing views, or even playing devil's advocate in discussions can ignite the critical faculties.

While tools and techniques are essential in the curation process, it's the spirit of critical thinking that truly breathes life into it. It ensures that the knowledge acquired is not just vast, but also deep, relevant, and rigorously vetted.

The Power of Deliberate Ignorance

In the age of information abundance, there's a counterintuitive notion that's gaining traction: sometimes, less is more. While our digital era offers unprecedented access to knowledge, it's equally important to recognize the value of deliberate ignorance. By consciously choosing what to engage with and what to let go, individuals can preserve their cognitive energy and enhance the quality of their knowledge acquisition.

Central to this approach is acknowledging the limits of our cognitive bandwidth. The human mind, incredible as it is, has finite processing power. With the constant barrage of information, it's easy to feel overwhelmed, leading to mental fatigue and diminished retention. By embracing deliberate ignorance, individuals ensure they don't spread themselves too thin and instead, focus on absorbing what truly matters.

Drawing parallels with nutrition, the concept of the "information diet" emerges. Just as one would be cautious about the food they consume, it's crucial to be discerning about the information ingested. This doesn't imply deprivation but emphasizes intentionality and moderation. A balanced information diet involves seeking out high-quality sources, taking breaks to digest and reflect, and avoiding the 'junk' that can clutter the mind.

Further deepening this philosophy is the shift from "just-in-case" learning to "just-in-time" learning. Traditional learning models often promote acquiring knowledge for potential future use, leading to a stockpile of information that may or may not be utilized. In contrast, the just-in-time approach encourages learning when it's immediately relevant and applicable. This ensures that information is fresh, contextually relevant, and can be integrated seamlessly into current projects or challenges.

While the vast reservoirs of digital knowledge present an incredible opportunity, it's equally crucial to recognize the power of strategic ignorance. By curating one's information intake, setting boundaries, and focusing on timely learning, individuals can navigate the digital age with clarity, purpose, and efficacy.

As we journey through the expansive universe of digital knowledge, it becomes increasingly evident that effective curation is not a passive endeavor but a proactive, intentional act. It's a dance of discernment, where every step, every pause, and every move is made with purpose.

Curation is akin to artistry. Just as an artist selects colors with precision and places each brushstroke with care, a curator too must weave through the vast tapestry of information, picking out threads that resonate most deeply. This art, however, is not merely about amassing volumes of knowledge but about ensuring that each piece chosen is meaningful and impactful.

This journey is less about the roads traveled and more about the footprints left behind. It's not the sheer volume of knowledge accessed, but the depth and richness of understanding that truly counts. Readers are encouraged to dive deep, to immerse themselves fully into areas of interest rather than skimming the surface. Depth over breadth becomes the guiding principle, ensuring that learning is not just expansive but also profound.

Moreover, in a world that often celebrates accumulation – be it wealth, possessions, or even information – we must shift our focus. It's not about how much we know but how well we understand. Knowledge without understanding is like a ship without a compass – it might look impressive but is directionless.

Thus, as we conclude this exploration into curation, the call to action is clear. Approach knowledge with intention, prioritize quality over quantity, seek understanding over mere accumulation, and above all, be the curator of your own learning journey, ensuring it's as enriching as it is enlightening.

Chapter 7:

Transforming Knowledge into Action

The Journey from Knowing to Doing

The divide between simply having knowledge and actively applying it is vast and, in many ways, significant. It's akin to the difference between having a toolbox and knowing how to proficiently use each tool inside. The former pertains to the possession, and the latter to proficiency.

In the vast digital landscapes we navigate daily, information abounds. The internet, with its libraries of e-books, articles, videos, and tutorials, has democratized access to information like never before. This incredible availability, while being a boon, has also given rise to a unique challenge. The sheer volume and accessibility of knowledge mean that possessing it isn't as unique or valuable as it once was. Today, the differentiation lies not in what you know, but in how you use what you know. This transition from knowing to doing is where many young professionals find their biggest hurdle.

Knowledge, by its nature, is passive. It rests in databases, books, and minds, waiting to be called upon. However, in our rapidly evolving world, passive knowledge is not enough. It must be converted into active, actionable intelligence to have any real-world impact. The term "actionable intelligence" may sound like it belongs in a spy thriller, but in essence, it relates to the capacity to turn information into effective actions. It's the difference between reading about market trends and using that understanding to steer a business in a profitable direction.

In today's dynamic world, actionable intelligence is indispensable. As markets shift, technologies evolve, and societal values transform, the ability to not just accumulate knowledge but to translate it into practical strategies becomes the key to success. Businesses don't thrive by merely understanding consumer needs; they prosper by meeting them. Scientists don't advance by only comprehending theories; they break boundaries by experimenting. Similarly, young professionals can't grow by merely accumulating degrees and reading books; they must be adept at translating their knowledge into tangible results.

The essence of actionable intelligence also underscores the need for adaptability. In a world characterized by flux, static knowledge rapidly becomes obsolete. Actionable intelligence is not just about using what you know but is also about continually updating, refining, and adapting that knowledge to meet new challenges and seize fresh opportunities.

As we delve deeper into this chapter, we'll explore strategies to bridge the gap between knowledge possession and knowledge application, helping young professionals equip themselves for success in the digital age. We'll investigate tools, mindsets, and methodologies that can empower individuals to transform static knowledge into dynamic solutions. Through real-world examples, practical exercises, and expert insights, we aim to provide a roadmap for mastering knowledge in action.

Synthesizing and Reflecting: Beyond Passive Consumption

In an era of information overload, the mere act of consuming knowledge can be overwhelming. Every day, countless articles, videos, podcasts, and e-books beckon for our attention. It's tempting to think that consuming more equates to knowing more. But the reality is, without the processes of synthesis and reflection, we might end up with a vast repository of fragmented facts that lack cohesion or context. Moving beyond passive consumption to a state where knowledge becomes truly integrated into our understanding requires conscious effort.

Synthesis plays a pivotal role in this transformation. Imagine you're piecing together a jigsaw puzzle. Each piece represents a separate piece of knowledge. On its own, each piece might be colorful and interesting, but it's only when they come together that a complete picture emerges.

Synthesis is the process of merging these diverse knowledge fragments to form cohesive insights. It requires identifying patterns, connecting dots, and forming relationships between seemingly unrelated information. When we synthesize, we're not just memorizing or repeating what we've learned; we're creating a new understanding by combining multiple sources of information.

Equally important is the act of reflection. Reflection is the deep thinking that allows us to internalize information. It provides the space for us to ask questions, challenge assumptions, and evaluate the relevance of what we've learned. By reflecting, we can place knowledge in the context of our own experiences and aspirations. It gives knowledge depth and personal meaning. Without reflection, facts might quickly fade from memory. But with it, they become integrated into our worldview.

So, how does one engage in synthesis and reflection effectively? There are several practical methods that can assist in this endeavor:

Mind Maps: A visual representation of information, mind maps allow individuals to organize and structure their knowledge. By creating branches for related ideas and connecting them in a visual format, one can easily identify patterns and relationships. Mind maps are particularly useful when trying to understand complex topics with many interrelated concepts.

Synthesis Notes: Going beyond traditional note-taking, synthesis notes require individuals to actively combine information from multiple sources. Instead of verbatim copying, the focus is on distillation and integration. For instance, after reading several articles on a topic, one might write a synthesis note that captures the overarching themes and insights, highlighting where different sources converge or diverge.

Reflection Journals: A reflection journal is a dedicated space for introspection. Here, one can record thoughts, reactions, and questions related to what they've learned. It's a tool for personal dialogue, where knowledge meets individual context. Over time, reflection journals can become a treasure trove of insights, showing one's evolution in understanding and perspective.

While the digital age provides us with unprecedented access to knowledge, it's essential to recognize that consumption alone isn't sufficient. To truly harness the power of information, young professionals must become adept at synthesizing diverse knowledge streams and reflecting on their learning. By doing so, they not only retain information better but also develop a deeper, more nuanced understanding of their chosen fields.

From Theory to Practice: Knowledge Application in Real-World Scenarios

One of the great challenges faced by professionals of all ages, but especially young ones entering the workforce, is the transition from theoretical knowledge to practical application. Understanding a concept in a controlled, educational environment is one thing; applying it in the unpredictable, multifaceted world of work is entirely another. However, this is where the true power and value of knowledge come to the fore.

Take the realm of business as an example. Understanding market theories, consumer behavior models, or financial principles is foundational. But it's in the real-world application – launching a product, engaging with customers, or making investment decisions – that these theories come alive and truly make a difference.

Using Case Studies to Illustrate Successful Knowledge Transfers

Case studies serve as a bridge between theory and practice. They present real-world situations where theoretical knowledge has been applied, with all the complexities, challenges, and nuances that come with it. By studying these cases, individuals can gain insights into how knowledge can be transferred from the pages of a textbook to the practicalities of professional life.

For instance, consider a case study about a company that turned around its fortunes by harnessing customer feedback. While the theories of customer centricity might be taught in classrooms, this case study will show how the company actively sought feedback, analyzed it, and then implemented changes in their product lineup or marketing strategies. The tangible results – increased sales, improved customer loyalty – provide a compelling illustration of theory put into effective action.

Contextual Adaptation: Modifying and Molding Knowledge to Fit Different Scenarios

Every situation, every challenge, is unique. Therefore, while foundational knowledge remains consistent, its application must be flexible. Contextual adaptation is the art and science of tweaking, modifying, and molding theoretical knowledge to fit the specific contours of a given scenario.

A financial principle, for instance, might need to be adapted differently for a startup than for a multinational corporation. Similarly, a marketing strategy effective in one cultural context might require adjustments in another. The ability to adapt knowledge contextually is a mark of a professional who doesn't just understand their field but also knows how to navigate its real-world intricacies.

Embracing Experimentation: The Value of Trial and Error in Knowledge Application

Lastly, it's essential to recognize that not every application of knowledge will yield success. And that's okay. There is immense value in trial and error. Experimentation – the act of testing, iterating, and learning – is at the heart of knowledge application.

Consider the world of technology. For every successful app or platform, there are countless prototypes, beta versions, and failed attempts. But each of these "failures" offers lessons, insights, and pathways to eventual success. Embracing experimentation means recognizing that mistakes are not just inevitable but invaluable. They provide feedback, highlight gaps in understanding, and pave the way for refinement.

As young professionals step out from the academic world into their careers, the challenge is not just to remember what they've learned but to apply, adapt, and experiment with that knowledge. It's a journey of continuous learning, where every situation offers an opportunity to transform theoretical knowledge into real-world impact.

Business Insights: Applying Knowledge for Professional Growth

In the modern business landscape, being knowledgeable isn't merely a plus —it's a prerequisite for success. But having knowledge and effectively applying it are two distinct skills. The former equips you with tools, while the latter determines how well you can wield them to sculpt your professional destiny. The arena of business offers a compelling stage to examine how knowledge can be translated into tangible growth, both for individuals and organizations.

Identifying Industry Trends Through Accumulated Knowledge

One of the most valuable uses of accumulated knowledge is in identifying and predicting industry trends. Professionals who can spot a nascent trend early can position themselves, and their businesses, to ride the wave of that trend, reaping significant rewards. This requires a deep understanding of the industry, a keen sense of observation, and the ability to synthesize information from various sources.

For instance, a marketer who has studied consumer behavior patterns, emerging technologies, and socio-economic shifts might identify a rising demand for sustainable products in a particular demographic. This insight could lead to the development of a new product line, tapping into an unmet need before competitors catch on.

Enhancing Decision-Making with Data and Research-Backed Knowledge

The era we live in is often referred to as the age of data. Data-driven decision-making is no longer a luxury; it's a necessity. But raw data, in isolation, is of limited use. It's the interpretation of this data, backed by research and knowledge, that turns it into a goldmine.

Imagine a company trying to decide on the launch location for a new retail outlet. Raw data might show high footfall in several potential locations. However, a professional equipped with knowledge about urban planning, local demographics, and consumer behavior can interpret this data to choose the best location. This decision, informed by knowledge and research, significantly increases the probability of the store's success.

Crafting Informed Strategies and Business Plans: From Ideation to Execution

A business strategy or plan isn't just a roadmap—it's a vision brought to life through actionable steps. The foundation of any successful strategy is knowledge. This encompasses understanding market dynamics, customer needs, competitive landscapes, regulatory environments, and much more.

A young entrepreneur, for instance, might have a groundbreaking product idea. But it's their knowledge of supply chain management, branding, distribution channels, and funding mechanisms that will turn this idea into a successful business venture. From the ideation phase, where market gaps are identified, to execution, where operations are rolled out, every step is infused with and guided by knowledge.

Crafting strategies also involves foreseeing potential challenges and being prepared with contingency plans. Here too, knowledge plays a crucial role. A professional who understands the cyclic nature of their industry, for example, will ensure that their business remains resilient during downturns.

In the world of business, knowledge is both the compass and the map. It points professionals in the right direction and guides them on their journey. As they climb the corporate ladder or build ventures from scratch, the ability to apply knowledge effectively becomes the cornerstone of their growth. In this ever-evolving landscape, it's the informed, agile, and knowledgeable professionals who stand out, driving progress not just for themselves but for the entire industry.

Techniques for Effective Brainstorming

Brainstorming has long been recognized as a powerful tool for generating ideas, solving problems, and fostering innovation. When done correctly, it can unleash a cascade of insights, leading to breakthrough solutions.

However, the process of brainstorming is not just about gathering people in a room and asking them to think. Effective brainstorming is structured, directed, and often facilitated by specific techniques that guide the ideation process. Here, we explore some of these techniques, each with its unique approach and benefits.

SCAMPER: A Mnemonic for Brainstorming

SCAMPER stands as a mnemonic that aids individuals and teams in asking questions and generating ideas. Each letter of the acronym represents a different thinking approach:

Substitute: What elements of the current situation or product can be replaced with something else? For instance, can a different material be used in a product to make it more eco-friendly.

Combine: Can you merge two or more elements to produce a better solution? For example, combining the features of a phone and a camera led to the rise of smartphones with high-quality imaging capabilities.

Adapt: How can you adjust or tweak the current situation to improve it? This could involve adapting features from another industry or context.

Modify: What can be magnified, enhanced, or added to the current situation? Could a service be modified to cater to a different demographic

Put to another use: Can the product or idea be used in a different context or for a different purpose? Think of how baking soda, initially used for baking, found its way into cleaning and personal care.

Eliminate: What can you remove or simplify? Often, less is more. For instance, eliminating a complicated step in a process might make it more user-friendly.

Reverse: Can you rearrange or invert any elements for better results? This could involve reversing the order of steps in a process or rethinking hierarchies.

SCAMPER acts as a checklist, ensuring that brainstorming sessions explore ideas from multiple angles, thereby increasing the chance of uncovering innovative solutions.

Brain writing: Silent Idea Generation Before Group Discussions

Traditional brainstorming often involves vocal participation, which can sometimes lead to louder voices dominating or ideas being prematurely judged. Brain writing offers a remedy. In this technique, participants silently write down their ideas before any group discussion begins. Each individual gets an uninterrupted space to think and jot down insights.

After a set time, these written ideas are shared, combined, and expanded upon in a group discussion. The advantage here is twofold: it ensures every voice is heard, and it often leads to a larger pool of ideas as individuals aren't influenced by early vocal suggestions.

The Six Thinking Hats: Diverse Thinking Modes for Comprehensive Brainstorming

Developed by Dr. Edward de Bono, the Six Thinking Hats method requires participants to adopt different "hats" or modes of thinking during a brainstorming session. Each hat represents a distinct perspective:

White Hat: Focuses on data and facts. What information do we have, and what do we need?

Red Hat: Centers on feelings, intuition, and emotions. How do we feel about the idea or situation?

Black Hat: Represents critical judgment. What are the potential problems or risks?

Yellow Hat: Brings forward optimism and positive judgment. What are the benefits and positives?

Green Hat: Encourages creativity and new ideas. What are some innovative approaches or solutions?

Blue Hat: Oversees the thinking process, ensuring the guidelines are followed, and objectives are met.

By systematically switching between these hats, groups can ensure that they view challenges and ideas from diverse angles, leading to well-rounded and comprehensive solutions.

In sum, effective brainstorming isn't an act of spontaneity but a structured process. By adopting techniques like SCAMPER, Brain writing, and the Six Thinking Hats, professionals can harness the collective intelligence of a group, transforming scattered thoughts into actionable insights.

Driving Innovation with Knowledge

Innovation is the lifeblood of progress in both the business world and society at large. At its core, innovation is about finding new ways to solve problems, meet needs, and add value. While many believe innovation stems from sporadic flashes of genius, in reality, it's deeply rooted in the accumulation, synthesis, and application of knowledge. This chapter delves into how knowledge acts as a catalyst for innovation, enabling professionals to spot opportunities, create groundbreaking solutions, and iterate upon them for perfection.

Recognizing Gaps and Needs in the Market Through Knowledge Synthesis

In the vast landscape of the market, opportunities often manifest as gaps or unmet needs. Identifying these requires a deep understanding of current market dynamics, consumer behaviors, technological advancements, and socio-economic patterns. By synthesizing knowledge from these areas, professionals can pinpoint where existing solutions fall short and where there's potential for innovation.

For instance, a professional well-versed in environmental science and consumer behavior might recognize a growing demand for sustainable alternatives to everyday products. This synthesis of knowledge helps them spot an opportunity to introduce biodegradable or recyclable alternatives that cater to the environmentally conscious segment of the market.

Merging Knowledge from Disparate Sources for Groundbreaking Innovations

The most groundbreaking innovations often emerge at the intersection of diverse fields. When knowledge from seemingly unrelated domains converges, it opens up avenues for solutions that might have been previously unimaginable.

Consider the rise of wearable health technology. It required a melding of expertise from medical science, digital technology, design, and user experience. Professionals who could integrate knowledge from all these areas were able to create devices that monitor health metrics in real-time, offering consumers insights and alerts right on their wrists.

In another example, the fusion of biotechnology with information technology has paved the way for personalized medicine, where treatments can be tailored to individual genetic profiles. These examples underline the potential of combining knowledge from different areas to craft novel solutions.

Iterative Feedback: Using Knowledge to Refine and Improve Innovative Solutions

No innovation is perfect at its inception. Once a new product, service, or solution is introduced, it requires refinement based on user feedback and changing market dynamics. Knowledge plays a pivotal role in this iterative process.

By gathering feedback, professionals gain insights into how their innovations function in real-world scenarios. This data, when combined with knowledge about the market, technology, and users, allows for continuous improvement. For instance, a new software application might undergo several updates post-launch, each one addressing bugs, improving user experience, or introducing new features based on the evolving needs of its user base.

It's important to note that this iterative process is not just about rectifying shortcomings but also about staying ahead of the curve. In today's rapidly changing world, what's innovative today can become obsolete tomorrow. Constantly updating one's knowledge and integrating feedback ensures that innovations remain relevant, effective, and ahead of the competition.

In conclusion, knowledge is not just a passive repository of information. It's an active force, driving professionals to challenge the status quo, spot opportunities, and craft solutions that redefine industries and enrich lives. In the realm of innovation, knowledge isn't just power; it's the engine of progress.

Nurturing a Knowledge-Driven Culture

In the realm of business and organizational dynamics, the culture that permeates a team or institution plays a pivotal role in shaping outcomes. While strategies, technologies, and markets are all important factors, it's often the intangible essence of culture that determines how effectively these elements are harnessed. A knowledge-driven culture, characterized by continuous learning, knowledge sharing, and the celebration of innovation, emerges as a powerful catalyst for growth and success. This chapter delves into how such a culture can be nurtured, sustained, and leveraged for organizational excellence.

Encouraging Continuous Learning and Application in Teams and Organizations

At the heart of a knowledge-driven culture lies the ethos of continuous learning. It's not just about acquiring information but also applying it in real-world contexts. Encouraging continuous learning requires more than just providing resources; it involves fostering an environment where curiosity is celebrated, questions are welcomed, and exploration is incentivized.

Leaders can facilitate this by introducing regular training sessions, workshops, and courses tailored to the needs of their teams. But beyond formal education, it's equally crucial to cultivate a mindset where professionals feel empowered to seek knowledge autonomously, be it through reading, online courses, or engaging with experts in the field.

Application complements acquisition. By providing platforms where team members can apply what they've learned—whether through internal projects, presentations, or brainstorming sessions—organizations not only reinforce learning but also benefit from fresh perspectives and solutions.

Knowledge Sharing as a Catalyst for Collective Growth

While individual learning is foundational, collective growth is accelerated when knowledge is shared across the organization. Knowledge sharing bridges the gaps between departments, reduces redundancy, and fosters a collaborative spirit.

Instituting regular knowledge-sharing sessions, where team members can present insights from their areas of expertise or recent learnings, can be immensely beneficial. Digital platforms, like intranet portals or knowledge management systems, can also be employed to create repositories of shared resources, best practices, and insights.

When knowledge flows freely within an organization, it creates a ripple effect. Challenges are addressed more holistically, solutions become more robust, and the entire organization operates with a unified, informed perspective.

Rewarding Innovation and Informed Risk-Taking in Business Settings

A knowledge-driven culture is not just about accumulation and dissemination; it's also about application in novel ways. Innovation and risk-taking, when informed by deep knowledge, can lead to breakthroughs that propel an organization forward.

However, for professionals to take these leaps, they must feel that their efforts will be recognized and rewarded. Celebrating successes, no matter how big or small, reinforces the value the organization places on innovative thinking. But it's equally crucial to recognize and learn from failures. When teams know that informed risks, even if they don't always lead to success, are appreciated, it fosters a culture of experimentation and exploration.

Furthermore, tangible rewards—be it in the form of bonuses, promotions, or other recognition's—signal to the team the tangible benefits of leveraging knowledge for innovation.

In essence, a knowledge-driven culture is more than just a buzzword; it's a strategic approach to organizational growth. By championing continuous learning, facilitating knowledge sharing, and celebrating innovation, organizations not only equip themselves to navigate the complexities of today's business landscape but also set the stage for continued success in the future.

Overcoming Barriers to Knowledge Application

As the age-old adage goes, "Knowledge is power." Yet, the acquisition of knowledge is merely the first step in a longer journey. The true value of knowledge lies in its application. However, even the most well-informed individuals and organizations can encounter barriers that prevent the effective utilization of what they know. From cognitive biases to the paralysis brought on by over-analysis, these obstacles can impede progress. This chapter delves into these challenges, offering insights into their origins and practical strategies to overcome them.

Addressing Cognitive Biases that Hinder Effective Action

Cognitive biases are systematic patterns of deviation from norm or rationality in judgment. They can cloud our perception, leading us to make decisions that aren't aligned with the available knowledge. Some common biases include confirmation bias (favoring information that confirms pre-existing beliefs), anchoring bias (relying heavily on the first piece of information encountered), and availability heuristic (relying on immediate examples that come to mind).

Overcoming these biases requires self-awareness. Professionals need to be trained to recognize when they might be falling prey to such biases. Encouraging diverse perspectives, seeking external feedback, and constantly challenging one's own assumptions are crucial steps in this direction. By creating a culture that values objective decision-making and is wary of potential biases, organizations can ensure that knowledge is applied in its truest, most effective form.

Combating Analysis Paralysis: Making Decisions When Overwhelmed with Information

In the digital age, with the sheer volume of information available, there's a risk of becoming overwhelmed, leading to what's termed "analysis paralysis." This state occurs when an individual or organization is so caught up in analyzing information that they become incapacitated, unable to make timely decisions.

To combat this, it's essential to have clear decision-making frameworks in place. These can include setting specific criteria for decisions, limiting the time available for certain choices, or employing tools that help in prioritizing information. For instance, the Pareto principle, or the 80/20 rule, suggests that 80% of effects come from 20% of causes. By focusing on this vital 20% of information, decision-makers can act more swiftly and effectively.

The Role of Emotional Intelligence in Navigating Knowledge Application

Emotional intelligence (EI) refers to the ability to recognize, understand, and manage our own emotions while also recognizing, understanding, and influencing the emotions of others. While it might seem unrelated, EI plays a crucial role in the application of knowledge. Knowledge isn't applied in a vacuum; it interacts with interpersonal dynamics, organizational cultures, and individual emotions.

A professional with high emotional intelligence can gauge the emotional undertones of a situation, tailoring the application of knowledge to fit the context. They can navigate resistance to change, persuade stakeholders, and foster an environment conducive to the acceptance of new ideas. By understanding the emotional landscapes of themselves and those around them, they can bridge the gap between what's known and what's done.

While knowledge offers immense potential, its true power is realized only when barriers to its application are acknowledged and overcome. By addressing cognitive biases, ensuring decisive action amidst information abundance, and leveraging emotional intelligence, professionals and organizations can ensure that knowledge translates into meaningful, impactful action.

As we conclude this exploration of knowledge in the digital age, it's imperative to circle back to a foundational truth: Knowledge, in and of itself, holds potential, but it's in the act of application that its true value emerges. This journey, from the acquisition of knowledge to its effective utilization, is not just about individual or organizational growth. It's about shaping a future that's informed, dynamic, and responsive to the changing contours of our world.

Re-emphasizing the Paramount Importance of Action in the Knowledge Journey

Throughout this discourse, one theme has been consistently echoed: the move from knowing to doing. Possessing vast amounts of information without the drive or capability to act upon it is akin to having a treasure trove locked away in a vault. The true richness of knowledge blossoms when it's set into motion, when it's used as a tool to innovate, to solve problems, to build bridges, and to chart out new territories. It's the action, the doing, the application that brings to life the dormant power of what we know.

Inspiring Readers to See Knowledge Not as an End, but as Fuel for Meaningful Change and Progress

As we stand at this juncture of unparalleled access to information, it's easy to view knowledge as a destination. The myriad sources, from digital libraries to online courses, can make it seem as though the ultimate goal is to accumulate as much as one can. However, this perspective needs a paradigm shift.

Knowledge isn't the final destination; it's the fuel for our journey. It's the spark that ignites innovation, the compass that guides decision-making, and the foundation upon which progress is built. In every fragment of knowledge, there lies the potential for change, for betterment, for evolution. And it's upon us, as professionals, as organizations, and as members of society, to harness this potential, to see knowledge not just as a static entity but as a dynamic force propelling us forward.

In wrapping up this chapter, the hope is that you, as the reader, are inspired to not just be a passive consumer of knowledge but an active participant in its journey. May you always be driven to learn, to understand, to question, and most importantly, to act. Because in the intricate dance between knowledge and action lies the rhythm of progress, the melody of innovation, and the heartbeat of a brighter future.

Chapter 8:
Sharing and Collaborating

The power of networked knowledge. Building a personal brand through knowledge sharing.

Collaborative tools and platforms for team-based knowledge management.

In an era where the flux of information is ceaseless, the act of solitary knowledge acquisition and application may no longer suffice. The paradigms of growth, innovation, and success have been redefined to encompass collaboration and sharing as pivotal components. The amplification of individual knowledge through collaborative synergies not only adds layers of depth and dimension but also spawns possibilities previously unimaginable. This chapter delves deep into the art and science of sharing knowledge and the transformative power of collaboration in the digital age.

The Power of Collective Wisdom

Across millennia, human progress has been underpinned by the sharing of knowledge. From the oral traditions of ancient civilizations to the global digital networks of today, sharing knowledge has bridged generational, geographical, and cultural divides, fostering an intricate tapestry of collective wisdom. The power of this collective wisdom surpasses the sum of its parts, enabling communities and organizations to leapfrog challenges, innovate, and adapt at an accelerated pace.

From Silos to Synergy: Breaking Boundaries in Knowledge Sharing

Modern organizations, despite their vast repositories of information, often grapple with knowledge silos—sections of an entity where sharing does not occur beyond the group. These silos stifle innovation, hinder adaptability, and suppress growth. Overcoming these barriers requires a strategic shift towards a culture that values open communication, transparent sharing, and cross-functional collaboration. Tools like collaborative platforms, knowledge management systems, and regular cross-departmental meetings can be instrumental in this transformation, turning isolated pockets of expertise into integrated hubs of shared wisdom.

The Digital Renaissance: Collaborative Platforms and Communities

The digital age has ushered in a renaissance of knowledge sharing and collaboration. Platforms like wikis, forums, and online communities enable individuals worldwide to collaborate on projects, solve complex problems, and share diverse perspectives. These platforms are more than mere repositories; they're vibrant ecosystems where knowledge is co-created, refined, and disseminated. They democratize information, allowing anyone, irrespective of their background or credentials, to contribute to the collective understanding.

Leveraging Collaborative Tools for Organizational Excellence

Within organizational settings, collaborative tools play a pivotal role in streamlining operations, fostering innovation, and enhancing productivity. Tools such as shared document editors, project management software, and virtual whiteboards empower teams to co-create, discuss, and refine ideas in real-time. By centralizing information and fostering transparent communication, these tools ensure that all stakeholders remain aligned, informed, and engaged.

The Ethos of Open Source and the Future of Collaboration

Open source, a philosophy rooted in the free and collaborative development of software, epitomizes the future of knowledge sharing and collaboration. By making source code accessible to all, it invites a global community to contribute, refine, and innovate. This ethos, though rooted in software, has profound implications for other domains. It challenges traditional notions of ownership, competition, and innovation, signaling a future where knowledge is not hoarded but shared, not guarded but celebrated.

In the Dance of Sharing and Collaborating, Lies the Symphony of Progress

As we reflect on the journey of sharing and collaborating, it becomes evident that the tapestry of human progress is woven with threads of shared wisdom, collective endeavors, and synergistic collaborations. In the dance of sharing knowledge, in the rhythms of collaborative efforts, we find the symphony of progress, the melody of innovation, and the promise of a future where knowledge is not just the domain of the few but the shared heritage of all.

Amplifying Impact through Collective Wisdom

As we traverse the digital age's vast landscapes, a powerful paradigm has emerged, reshaping how we perceive knowledge. No longer is knowledge seen merely as an individual's intellectual reservoir; it has transformed into a collective conduit, magnifying the impact of every piece of information shared. This shift is not just an evolution; it's a revolution that underscores the unparalleled potential of collective wisdom.

The Multiplier Effect of Shared Knowledge

Imagine a singular spark. On its own, it flickers and shines, a beacon of its own existence. Now, envision that spark igniting countless others, each building upon the brilliance of the one before. This is the essence of the multiplier effect that shared knowledge brings. Every time knowledge is shared, it doesn't diminish; instead, it expands, influences, and multiplies. Each individual or organization it touches becomes equipped to act, innovate, or further share, creating a ripple effect of growth and impact. This is the potency of collective wisdom - it doesn't merely add; it amplifies.

Knowledge Not as a Limited Resource, but as a Catalyst for Community and Growth

There's a prevalent misconception that treats knowledge like a finite resource, where sharing might mean losing. But, much like love or joy, knowledge grows when it's disseminated. It becomes the bridge connecting diverse minds, fostering community, and sparking collaboration. Each shared insight or piece of information serves as a catalyst, propelling forward both the sharer and the recipient.

By embracing knowledge as a catalyst, we shift from a mindset of scarcity to one of abundance. Communities, be they professional, academic, or creative, thrive when knowledge flows freely. They become hotbeds of innovation, where ideas are not hoarded but nurtured, refined, and expanded upon collectively. In such an environment, growth is not just linear; it's exponential.

As we embark on this exploration of sharing and collaborating, it's essential to recognize that knowledge, in its truest essence, is not meant to be kept in silos. It yearns to flow, to connect, to multiply. And in that journey of knowledge, from the mind of one to the hearts of many, lies the promise of a world that's not just more informed, but more connected, more innovative, and infinitely more enriched.

The Power of Networked Knowledge

In our increasingly interconnected world, we are witnessing the ascent of networked knowledge. This phenomenon reaches beyond the confines of individual expertise and crafts an intricate tapestry of insights, experiences, and understandings. It's an exploration of the dynamic symphony of diverse knowledge nodes harmonizing together, culminating in an emergent wisdom that's deeper and all-encompassing.

Understanding the concept of a "knowledge network" unveils a vast web. Here, every node symbolizes the knowledge of an individual or entity, and the threads connecting them represent channels of communication and collaboration. This network thrives on the richness of diversity, seamless connectivity, and the spirit of open sharing. The beauty of such a structure lies in its promise of diverse thought. As knowledge from varied sources converges, it offers an array of perspectives, facilitating holistic solutions. The network also ensures that information courses through its veins at an impressive speed, making rapid dissemination of ideas and innovations a reality. This interwoven knowledge web becomes a cradle for innovation. The meeting of myriad expertise gives birth to collaborative endeavors where ideas cross paths, mingle, and elevate each other. Furthermore, the resilience of such a structure is noteworthy. In a networked knowledge system, the dependency on a singular source is minimized. If a node encounters setbacks, the network displays a chameleonic adaptability, relying on the collective strength of other nodes to maintain the uninterrupted flow of information.

Networked knowledge has left indelible marks across industries and communities. Consider the realm of open-source software. Platforms like GitHub stand as testaments to the prowess of knowledge networks. Developers spanning continents converge on such platforms, pooling their expertise to forge software that is not only robust but continuously evolving. Another beacon of collective intelligence is Wikipedia. Here, a global community of contributors pour in their insights, editing and refining entries, ensuring a dynamic and up-to-date reservoir of knowledge. Even the academic world isn't untouched. Collaborative networks like ResearchGate bridge researchers, offering them platforms to share their discoveries, partner on groundbreaking studies, and constructively build upon each other's work.

Yet, at the core of this intricate dance of networked knowledge is a principle of balance. It's a dance between giving and receiving. Participants in this network play dual roles. They are contributors, pouring in their unique insights, and simultaneously beneficiaries, drawing from the collective well of wisdom. This relationship isn't just transactional but symbiotic, ensuring the network's vibrancy and sustainability. The very act of sharing in such a system is layered with significance. It not only adds to the collective intelligence but simultaneously strengthens individual reputations, cements authority, and weaves threads of meaningful connections.

In essence, networked knowledge isn't just a modern marvel; it's a testament to the collective spirit of humanity, where shared wisdom paves the path for a future brimming with possibilities.

Building a Personal Brand through Knowledge Sharing

In the vast expanse of the digital age, where information abounds and attention is a premium, the concept of a personal brand has ascended to prominence. Within the bustling realms of the knowledge economy, your personal brand is not just about who you are or what you do, but more critically, about the value you bring, the insights you offer, and the wisdom you share.

Understanding personal branding in the context of the knowledge economy is akin to recognizing oneself as a distinct entity, a unique knowledge hub. It's about carving a niche where your expertise, experiences, and insights converge, making you an entity of value and relevance. It's no longer about just having a specific skill set; it's about the narrative, the stories, and the insights that surround those skills, and how they can benefit, inform, or inspire others.

To position oneself as a thought leader in a niche or industry requires a blend of authenticity, consistency, and strategic visibility. Authenticity ensures that your personal brand is rooted in genuine knowledge and passion. It's about being true to your insights, experiences, and expertise, ensuring that what you share resonates with credibility. Consistency, on the other hand, is about regular engagement, continuous learning, and persistent sharing. It's about being present, active, and involved in discussions, debates, and dialogues that pertain to your niche. Strategic visibility involves making calculated moves to ensure that your knowledge reaches the right audience. This might involve collaborations, guest appearances, or leveraging platforms that cater to your target demographic.

In today's digital landscape, myriad platforms and channels beckon, each offering unique advantages for knowledge dissemination. Blogs stand as a testament to the written word's power, offering a space for detailed analysis, storytelling, and expertise sharing. They are the digital diaries where thoughts crystallize and knowledge is archived for eager seekers. Podcasts, with their audio centric approach, have emerged as the new radio, providing listeners with nuanced discussions, interviews, and deep dives into niche topics, all at their convenience. Webinars offer an interactive avenue, bridging experts with an audience in real-time, facilitating discussions, Q&A sessions, and live demonstrations. Additionally, platforms like YouTube for videos, LinkedIn for professional insights, Twitter for quick updates, and Instagram for visual storytelling, each offer avenues to not just share knowledge but to shape perceptions, influence discussions, and build a community around one's personal brand.

Building a personal brand through knowledge sharing is not just a strategic endeavor; it's a journey. A journey of continuous learning, authentic sharing, and meaningful engagements. In the knowledge economy, your personal brand becomes your beacon, guiding those seeking insights, inspiration, or expertise to your digital doorstep.

Social Learning: Peer-to-Peer Knowledge Exchange

Amidst traditional educational frameworks, there emerges a powerful paradigm that hinges on collaboration, interaction, and mutual growth: social learning. Rooted deeply in the ethos that we, as individuals, learn best within communal contexts, social learning underscores the significance of observing, interacting, and modeling behaviors, attitudes, and emotional reactions of others.

The educational philosophy behind social learning traces its roots to several psychological and pedagogical theories. Central to this philosophy is the idea that learning is inherently social and that our understanding of the world is shaped through our interactions with peers, mentors, and the broader community. This perspective posits that knowledge isn't a static entity to be transferred from an all-knowing entity to a passive receiver, but rather, it's dynamic, evolving, and co-constructed through social interactions.

The advantages of peer-based learning are manifold and profound. One of the most evident benefits is the introduction of diverse perspectives. Every individual, with their unique experiences, backgrounds, and worldviews, brings a fresh lens to the table, enriching discussions, and broadening horizons. This diversity fosters an environment where ideas are challenged, refined, and expanded upon, leading to a deeper, multifaceted understanding of subjects. Another pivotal advantage is the immediacy of real-time feedback. As peers engage, they offer instant responses, critiques, and suggestions, fostering an iterative learning process where ideas are continuously honed. Beyond just the academic or professional benefits, peer-based learning plays a pivotal role in community building. As individuals learn from and with each other, they forge bonds, establish trust, and cultivate a sense of belonging, transforming isolated learning journeys into collective quests for knowledge.

Illustrating the efficacy of peer-to-peer learning, several case studies stand out from both business and educational realms. In the corporate world, many organizations have embraced internal mentorship programs, where seasoned professionals guide newer employees, facilitating a two-way knowledge exchange. Such initiatives not only speed up onboarding processes but also foster a culture of continuous learning and collaboration. On the educational front, universities and schools worldwide have experimented with peer-led team learning (PLTL). In these setups, student leaders guide small groups through challenging coursework. The results have often showcased improved academic performance, enhanced understanding of concepts, and heightened engagement levels among participants.

In essence, social learning, with its peer-to-peer knowledge exchange, offers a promising alternative to traditional learning models. By emphasizing collaboration, mutual growth, and community, it reminds us that the journey of learning is as much about the connections we forge as it is about the knowledge we acquire.

Collaborative Tools for Team-Based Knowledge Management

In the digital era, as organizations scatter across the globe and remote work becomes a norm, the need for effective and efficient team-based knowledge management tools has never been more paramount. These tools, designed to streamline communication, foster collaboration, and centralize knowledge, have transformed the ways teams function, interact, and deliver.

Slack stands as a beacon of modern communication. Beyond its chat functionalities, it offers channels for topic-specific discussions, direct messaging for private conversations, and integration capabilities with a plethora of other tools and services. Slack ensures that communication is not just instantaneous but also organized. Teams can share files, seek feedback, and even integrate bots to automate specific tasks, ensuring that knowledge sharing happens in real-time and remains accessible.

Trello and Asana have carved a niche in the realm of project management. Both platforms, albeit with different user interfaces, focus on visual task management. While Trello thrives on card-based boards where tasks move through columns symbolizing stages, Asana offers more layout options, including lists, boards, and timelines. Both tools embed knowledge components seamlessly. Users can attach files, provide descriptions, set deadlines, and tag colleagues, ensuring that the entirety of a project's knowledge is centralized and accessible.

Confluence, a product of Atlassian, serves as a collaborative documentation platform. Whether it's for creating internal wikis, product documentation, or meeting notes, Confluence provides teams with a space to co-create content. Its rich-text editor, templates, and integration capabilities ensure that documentation becomes a collaborative effort, and knowledge is systematically archived and easily retrievable.

Google Workspace, formerly G Suite, presents a suite of cloud-based collaboration tools, covering documents, sheets, slides, and more. The real magic of Google Workspace lies in its seamless integration and real-time collaboration features. Multiple users can work on a single document simultaneously, witnessing live edits, commenting for feedback, and even chatting within the document. Such real-time interactions ensure that knowledge creation and refinement become a communal effort, reducing iterations and amplifying efficiency.

Lastly, GitHub has redefined collaborative software development. At its core, GitHub is a platform for version control, allowing developers to track changes, collaborate on code, and merge contributions from multiple sources. But beyond its technical prowess, GitHub has emerged as a hub for open-source knowledge sharing. Developers worldwide contribute to public repositories, sharing their code, insights, and innovations. This collective effort not only propels software development but also fosters a community where knowledge is freely shared, reviewed, and improved upon.

The landscape of team-based knowledge management has undergone a paradigm shift with these collaborative tools. As the boundaries of offices dissolve, these platforms ensure that teams remain connected, knowledge remains accessible, and collaboration remains uninterrupted. They symbolize the very spirit of the digital age: interconnected, dynamic, and knowledge-driven.

The Ethics of Knowledge Sharing

The digital age has democratized access to knowledge, ushering in an era of unparalleled information exchange. However, as with all revolutions, the rise of knowledge sharing comes with its own set of ethical quandaries. Central to these concerns are the principles of intellectual property rights, accurate representation, and the delicate balance between open-source generosity and safeguarding proprietary knowledge.

When it comes to knowledge sharing, intellectual property, and knowledge attribution stand at the forefront of ethical considerations. In an age where information flows seamlessly across digital platforms, it's crucial to recognize and respect the origins of ideas, theories, and creations. Properly attributing knowledge not only safeguards the rights of original creators but also maintains the integrity of shared content. Every piece of knowledge has a lineage, a history, and by honoring its source, we preserve its authenticity and value.

Paralleled, the tug-of-war between open-source sharing and proprietary knowledge protection continues to challenge individuals and organizations alike. Open-source ideals champion the free distribution of knowledge, emphasizing community-driven improvements and unrestricted access. This philosophy has birthed innovations, fostered communal growth, and propelled sectors like software development into new frontiers. However, there's also a legitimate need to protect proprietary knowledge, especially when it encompasses trade secrets, unique methodologies, or specialized research. Striking the right balance involves discerning what can be shared for collective benefit and what should be retained for competitive advantage or privacy.

Furthermore, the ease with which knowledge is disseminated today comes with the inherent responsibility of ensuring its accuracy. In a world where false information can spread like wildfire, it's incumbent upon knowledge sharers to verify, validate, and ensure that the content they propagate is factual, well-researched, and devoid of misleading elements. The repercussions of sharing incorrect or manipulated knowledge can range from mere misinformation to grave consequences in areas like health, finance, or public safety. Hence, responsibility in knowledge sharing isn't just an ethical mandate; it's a societal obligation.

Navigating these ethical waters of knowledge sharing requires a deep sense of responsibility, a respect for origins and rights, and a commitment to authenticity. As we continue to share, learn, and grow in this digital realm, it's essential to remember that with great access comes great responsibility. Our approach to knowledge, in sharing and in receiving, will shape the future landscapes of innovation, growth, and progress.

Embracing a Culture of Collaboration

The proliferation of the digital age, paired with the increasingly interconnected global landscape, has ushered organizations into recognizing that knowledge doesn't thrive in isolation. Instead, it blossoms when ideas intermingle, perspectives converge, and insights are co-created. Hence, the call for a collaborative culture has never been more resonant.

Building a collaborative mindset within teams and organizations begins with fostering an environment where every voice is valued, where diverse perspectives are not just tolerated but actively sought. It's about moving away from silos of expertise and instead, creating cross-functional teams where knowledge flows freely. This doesn't mean dismissing the importance of specialized skills. Instead, it emphasizes the belief that when diverse skills and knowledge bases come together, they result in richer, more comprehensive solutions.

Central to cultivating this collaborative ethos is leadership. Leaders wield the power to set the tone, establish norms, and, most importantly, lead by example. When leaders champion knowledge sharing initiatives, be it through open forums, team brainstorming sessions, or even casual knowledge-sharing lunches, they send a clear message about the value they place on collective wisdom. Furthermore, leadership's role isn't just about initiating such practices but also about rewarding them. Recognizing and celebrating instances of effective collaboration and knowledge sharing reinforces their importance and encourages more of such behavior.

The merits of a knowledge-sharing culture are manifold. Firstly, there's innovation. When minds meet, ideas collide, and from these collisions, emerge fresh solutions, novel approaches, and groundbreaking innovations. Collaboration often leads to 'Eureka' moments that solitary pondering may not yield. Secondly, there's an undeniable uptick in efficiency. With transparent communication and pooled resources, redundancy reduces, tasks get streamlined, and decision-making accelerates. Finally, and perhaps most importantly, there's a significant boost to employee engagement. When individuals feel that they are part of a larger conversation, when they see their insights being valued and their knowledge contributing to collective achievements, their sense of belonging and motivation soars.

Thus, embracing a culture of collaboration isn't just a progressive organizational strategy; it's a journey towards harnessing the full potential of collective intelligence. In this collaborative dance of minds, organizations not only achieve their immediate goals but also lay the foundation for sustainable growth and continuous evolution.

Challenges and Solutions in Collaborative Knowledge Management

The digital paradigm shift has made collaborative knowledge management both an essential organizational practice and a challenging endeavor. As with all transformative processes, it is accompanied by a set of unique challenges that require astute solutions. From information security concerns to resistance from team members and the ever-present danger of information silos, the road to effective collaborative knowledge management is fraught with obstacles. Yet, with the right strategies, these challenges can be transformed into stepping stones for even more effective collaboration.

Navigating the complex world of information security is paramount, especially when utilizing shared platforms. In a collaborative environment, information often flows across various channels, making it susceptible to breaches or unauthorized access. The solution lies in a combination of advanced technology and user training. On the technology front, it's crucial to invest in secure platforms that come with robust encryption, multi-factor authentication, and regular security updates. Simultaneously, team members must be educated about best practices, like strong password hygiene, recognizing phishing attempts, and the importance of regular software updates. By merging technology with awareness, information security becomes an integrated part of the collaborative process.

Resistance to collaborative tools and practices often stems from a mixture of unfamiliarity and the innate human reluctance to change. To overcome this, it's essential to prioritize training and orientation sessions. Instead of merely introducing a new tool, organizations should elucidate its benefits, demonstrate its ease of use, and highlight how it can make tasks more efficient. Change management strategies can be employed, which could include hands-on workshops, peer mentoring, or even gamified learning modules. The key is to ensure that the transition isn't seen as a forced imposition but rather as a beneficial progression.

Information silos, a challenge as old as organizational structures themselves, become even more pronounced in the digital age. These silos impede the free flow of knowledge and can lead to redundancies, miscommunications, and missed opportunities. To prevent them, streamlining communication is essential. This could be achieved by creating centralized knowledge repositories accessible to all relevant team members or implementing regular cross-departmental meetings to share updates and insights. Collaboration tools that offer integrations with other platforms can also be particularly helpful. These integrations ensure that information from different sources flows into a unified space, making access and retrieval more streamlined.

In essence, while the path to collaborative knowledge management may present challenges, they are not insurmountable. With a proactive approach, grounded in understanding and addressing the root causes of these challenges, organizations can pave the way for a collaborative culture that not only manages knowledge effectively but also leverages it for transformative growth and innovation.

The journey through collaborative knowledge management is akin to observing the magic that arises when individual sparks converge to create a roaring flame. Individual knowledge, with its depth and nuances, is a powerful entity. Yet, when it melds with collective wisdom, its potential magnifies exponentially. This synergistic potential is the beating heart of collaboration – where the sum is indeed greater than its parts.

Throughout history, humankind's greatest achievements have often been born out of collaboration. From scientific discoveries to transformative societal changes, when minds come together, boundaries are pushed, and new horizons are discovered. The digital era has expanded this collaborative space, transcending physical boundaries and creating a global knowledge-sharing ecosystem. Within this vast expanse, every piece of information, every insight, and every shared experience contributes to an intricate web of wisdom.

As we reflect on this immense potential, it's not just an invitation but a clarion call for readers to step into this ecosystem, not as passive observers but as active participants. The act of sharing knowledge is not a mere transfer of information but a gift that can enlighten, inspire, and empower. It's an opportunity to leave imprints, to contribute to the ever-evolving tapestry of global understanding.

In the grand scheme of things, every individual, with their unique experiences and insights, is a vital node in this vast network. And as we share, collaborate, and co-create, we're not just enriching ourselves but also shaping the future of knowledge, innovation, and progress. It's a journey where every contribution matters, and every collaboration brings us one step closer to a world bound by shared wisdom and collective growth.

Chapter 9:

Overcoming PKM Challenges

Navigating the Bumps on the Knowledge Road

Every pursuit, especially one as intricate and vast as managing one's personal knowledge, comes with its unique set of challenges. Embarking on the journey of Personal Knowledge Management (PKM) is like setting out on an enlightening road trip through the vast landscapes of information, learning, and growth. But like all road trips, while the destination and the journey itself can be exhilarating, there are inevitable bumps and detours along the way.

The very essence of PKM lies in its name, it's personal. This means that while there are standard challenges that many face, the individual nature of each person's knowledge journey brings its own set of hurdles. Over the years, the concept of PKM has evolved remarkably. In its nascent stages, PKM was predominantly seen as a system of organizing and retrieving information effectively. Think of it as a sophisticated filing cabinet where everything had its place. However, as the digital revolution surged forward and the sheer volume and accessibility of information exploded, it became evident that PKM was destined for a more profound purpose.

Today, PKM isn't just about managing information; it's about managing oneself in the realm of information. It's no longer solely about what you know but how you integrate what you know into who you are and how you grow. The challenges, therefore, aren't just technical or organizational. They're also deeply psychological and philosophical. For instance, in the face of endless information, how does one discern what's worth knowing? With countless tools at one's disposal, which ones align best with individual learning styles? And amid the constant barrage of new data, how does one find the time and mental space for reflection and deeper understanding?

As we delve into this chapter, we'll explore these challenges and many more. We'll unearth not just the problems but also the strategies and solutions that can help smooth out the bumps on the knowledge road. Most importantly, we'll recognize that these challenges aren't roadblocks but rather signposts, guiding us towards a more enlightened and effective PKM practice, one that not only enhances our information management but also fosters holistic personal growth.

Addressing Common Hurdles in PKM

The path to mastering Personal Knowledge Management is filled with challenges that, while daunting, are surmountable. Let's delve into some of the most prevalent hurdles and explore strategies to tackle them head-on.

Time Constraints: In an era where time seems perennially scarce, dedicating chunks of it to PKM can often feel overwhelming. How does one find the time amid work, personal commitments, and the myriad distractions of the digital age? The answer lies in being proactive about carving out dedicated knowledge time. Techniques such as time blocking, where specific blocks are reserved for PKM activities, can be instrumental. Similarly, the Pomodoro Technique, which involves working in focused sprints with regular breaks, can maximize productivity during these blocks. However, it's not just about finding time; it's also about seamlessly integrating PKM into one's daily life. This might mean listening to an educational podcast during a commute or setting aside the first 10 minutes of the day for knowledge reflection. Central to all these strategies is the need to have clear PKM goals. By understanding what you aim to achieve with your PKM endeavors, you can ensure that your time investment is always purpose-driven and impactful.

Tool Fatigue: The digital age, with its constant barrage of new apps and platforms, presents a unique challenge: tool fatigue. It's easy to be lured by the "shiny new tool" syndrome, where every new platform seems like the ultimate PKM solution. However, frequently jumping between tools can disrupt workflows and hinder genuine progress. The solution isn't to shun new tools but to be discerning about which ones genuinely align with individual needs and workflows. Before adopting a new tool, it's worth asking: Does this genuinely serve my PKM goals, or is it merely a distraction? Additionally, it's crucial to periodically evaluate the tools in use. If a tool no longer serves its purpose or becomes cumbersome, it might be time for a change. But remember, the best tool is often the one you'll consistently use.

Information Overload: If there's one word that defines the modern age, it's "more." More articles, more videos, more courses – an endless stream of information, which, while exciting, can be paralyzing. Navigating this deluge requires a keen sense of discernment. Start by filtering and prioritizing information sources. Not every article deserves a read, and not every video warrants a watch. This selective approach gives birth to the art of intentional ignorance, recognizing that sometimes, the power lies in choosing what to ignore. After all, our mental bandwidth is limited, and we must populate it with information that truly matters. To aid in this discernment, various tools and strategies can be employed for efficient information digestion and archiving. Whether it's using apps that highlight key takeaways from articles or maintaining a curated digital library, the goal is to transform the torrent of information into a manageable stream that fuels growth without overwhelming the senses.

The Mental Health Dimension: Knowledge Intake and Well-being

In our zealous quest for knowledge, it's easy to overlook an essential aspect of our existence: our mental health. The relentless pursuit of information and understanding can, paradoxically, lead to cognitive and emotional exhaustion, making it imperative to consider the intersection of knowledge intake and mental well-being.

Recognizing the Cognitive and Emotional Toll of Information Saturation: The human brain, while remarkable in its capacity, isn't inexhaustible. The continuous intake of information, especially in today's digital age, can saturate our cognitive abilities, leading to decision fatigue, reduced comprehension, and even burnout. Moreover, the nature of the information we consume, especially when it's negative or distressing, can have profound emotional ramifications. It can lead to feelings of anxiety, helplessness, or general unease. Hence, it's not just about how much we know but also about being cognizant of how this knowledge impacts our mental state.

Mindfulness Practices for a More Intentional and Balanced Knowledge Journey: Amidst this inundation, mindfulness emerges as a beacon. Mindfulness, at its core, is about being present, intentional, and non-judgmental. Applying this to our knowledge journey means consuming information with intent, understanding why we are seeking certain knowledge, and recognizing when to stop. It's about savoring each piece of information, reflecting upon its significance, and assimilating it in a way that's enriching rather than overwhelming. Simple practices like meditative reading, where one reads slowly and with full focus, or taking mindful breaks between learning sessions can be transformative.

Setting Boundaries: Digital Detox, Designated Quiet Times, and the Importance of Rest in Assimilation: As crucial as it is to absorb information, it's equally vital to know when to disconnect. A digital detox, which involves intentionally refraining from electronic devices and online platforms for a set period, can be a refreshing pause, allowing the mind to reset. Similarly, designating quiet times daily, be it through meditation, journaling, or simply being in nature, provides the mental space needed for deeper reflection and assimilation. And never underestimate the power of rest. The subconscious mind works wonders during periods of rest, making connections, and gaining insights that active learning might overlook. Sleep, in particular, plays a pivotal role in memory consolidation, underscoring its importance in any knowledge journey.

While the quest for knowledge is noble and enriching, it's essential to approach it with a sense of balance. By recognizing the signs of mental exhaustion, integrating mindfulness into our learning routines, and setting clear boundaries, we can ensure that our pursuit of knowledge complements our well-being rather than compromises it.

Balancing Breadth with Depth

In the digital age, where information is available at our fingertips and content is churned out at an unprecedented pace, we often find ourselves navigating the delicate balance between breadth and depth in our knowledge pursuits.

The Challenge of Surface-Level Knowledge in the Era of Rapid Content Consumption:
The vastness of the internet, combined with the fleeting nature of social media content, often nudges us towards a pattern of rapid, surface-level content consumption. The downside? While we might be aware of many topics, our understanding of them can remain shallow. Surface-level knowledge, although vast, often lacks the richness, nuance, and comprehension that deep knowledge brings. This superficiality can hamper critical thinking, problem-solving, and genuine expertise.

Strategies for Deep Dives: How and When to Invest in Depth:
While it's beneficial to be a jack-of-all-trades in some scenarios, there are times and situations where depth of knowledge becomes crucial. To foster this depth, one can employ various strategies. Deliberate practice, where one focuses on honing a particular skill or understanding a specific topic in depth, is a start. Setting aside dedicated time blocks, free from distractions, and engaging with primary sources or hands-on projects can further enhance understanding. Moreover, diving deep requires patience and perseverance, understanding that mastery or profound understanding doesn't come overnight.

The T-Shaped Knowledge Model: A Blend of Broad Horizons and Deep Expertise:
A popular concept in today's knowledge discourse is the T-shaped knowledge model. Picture the letter 'T'. The horizontal bar represents a broad understanding across many subjects, whereas the vertical bar signifies depth in a particular domain. This model suggests that while

having a wide range of knowledge is advantageous for cross-disciplinary thinking and versatility, possessing deep expertise in at least one area is equally essential. The deep expertise allows for innovation and leadership in that domain, while the broader knowledge facilitates communication, collaboration, and adaptability across different fields.

Striving for breadth and depth is not mutually exclusive. By recognizing the value of both, and by mindfully choosing when to skim and when to dive deep, individuals can cultivate a holistic and well-rounded knowledge portfolio, ready to tackle the diverse challenges of our modern world.

Strategies for Regular PKM System Reviews and Updates

In the realm of Personal Knowledge Management (PKM), the only constant is change. As we encounter new information, methodologies, and tools, it becomes imperative to periodically review and update our PKM systems to ensure they remain relevant and efficient. Here are some strategic approaches to make this process systematic and effective.

The Power of Reflection: Setting Aside Time for Monthly or Quarterly PKM Audits:
Reflection acts as the compass of our PKM journey. By consciously setting aside dedicated time, be it monthly or quarterly, for PKM audits, we can assess the effectiveness of our current practices. This practice not only helps in identifying areas of improvement but also celebrates successes and milestones achieved. It's akin to a health check-up for the PKM system, ensuring its robustness and relevance.

Feedback Loops: Using Personal Milestones and External Inputs to Refine the System:
Feedback, both internal and external, is invaluable. Personal milestones can provide insights into which strategies are bearing fruit. On the other hand, external inputs, be it from peers, mentors, or community forums, offer a fresh perspective. By creating a feedback loop, one ensures that the PKM system is not functioning in isolation but is continually refined based on results and collective wisdom.

Adaptive Evolution: Embracing Change and Growth in the PKM Journey:
PKM isn't a static endeavor. As we evolve in our personal and professional lives, our PKM system should mirror that growth. Whether it's integrating a new tool, updating methodologies, or discarding outdated information, adaptive evolution ensures that our PKM journey remains dynamic, responsive, and aligned with our ever-changing needs.

Checklists and Review Templates: Structured Tools to Guide Consistent PKM Evaluations:
To streamline the review process, structured tools like checklists and templates can be a boon. They offer a systematic approach to evaluations, ensuring that no aspect of the PKM system is overlooked. By following a set template, one can ensure consistency across reviews, making it easier to track progress and improvements over time.

In essence, regular reviews and updates are the lifeblood of an effective PKM system. They ensure that the system remains agile, responsive, and in tune with an individual's evolving needs and goals. By integrating these strategies, we ensure that our PKM remains a potent tool in our quest for lifelong learning and personal growth.

Overcoming Resistance and Procrastination

Navigating the expansive seas of knowledge can often feel overwhelming, and this sensation can introduce resistance and procrastination, two formidable adversaries in one's PKM journey. While these challenges are common, understanding their roots and having strategies to address them can significantly bolster our PKM endeavors.

Psychological Barriers in Knowledge Management: Fear, Overwhelm, and the Imposter Syndrome:
At the heart of resistance often lie deep-seated psychological barriers. Fear of not being able to effectively manage or retain vast amounts of information can be paralyzing. This fear, coupled with the sheer volume of information we often encounter, leads to feelings of overwhelm. Moreover, the impostor syndrome, a pervasive feeling of self-doubt or being a fraud despite evidence to the contrary, can further hamper one's motivation to

engage with and manage knowledge. Acknowledging these feelings and understanding that they're common experiences for many can be the first step toward addressing them.

Strategies to Build Momentum: Small Wins, Accountability Partnerships, and Visual Progress Trackers:
Counteracting resistance and procrastination requires both psychological and tactical approaches. Initiating with 'small wins' can be incredibly beneficial. By breaking down tasks into manageable portions and celebrating minor achievements, one can build momentum and confidence. Think of it as a snowball effect, where each small success leads to greater motivation and drive.

Accountability partnerships provide another layer of motivation. By partnering with a colleague, friend, or mentor, and sharing your PKM goals, you commit to a system of mutual encouragement and progress checks. This shared journey can make the process more engaging and provide the necessary nudge during moments of inertia.

Lastly, visual progress trackers, be it digital tools or physical charts, can offer a tangible representation of one's journey. Seeing one's progress visualized can be immensely motivating and serves as a constant reminder of the strides already taken and the goals ahead.

While resistance and procrastination might be natural reactions to the challenges of PKM, they're not insurmountable. By understanding the underlying psychological barriers and equipping oneself with effective strategies, one can navigate these hurdles and ensure that their PKM journey remains on a steadfast path.

Leveraging Community and External Support

The journey of personal knowledge management, while inherently personal, doesn't have to be a solitary one. By tapping into the wider community and seeking external support, individuals can significantly enrich their PKM experience, drawing from collective wisdom and shared experiences.

Joining PKM focused Groups and Forums for Shared Insights and Motivation:

In this digital age, there are countless platforms where like-minded individuals come together to discuss and share their experiences related to PKM. These forums and groups offer a treasure trove of insights, best practices, and solutions to common challenges. Beyond the tangible tips and tricks, being part of such a community can be a source of motivation. Knowing that there are others on a similar journey, facing similar challenges, can foster a sense of camaraderie and mutual support.

Attending Workshops, Webinars, and Courses to Continuously Refine PKM Skills:

The landscape of PKM is continuously evolving, with new tools, strategies, and philosophies emerging. By attending workshops, webinars, and courses, individuals can stay abreast of these developments, ensuring that their PKM system remains current and effective. Such formal learning environments also offer the chance to engage with experts in the field and glean insights from their experiences.

The Potential of Mentorship and Coaching in Overcoming PKM Challenges:

For those seeking more personalized guidance, mentorship and coaching can be invaluable. A mentor, having traversed the path of PKM, can offer tailored advice, strategies, and feedback. This one-on-one interaction can help in pinpointing specific challenges and crafting bespoke solutions. Moreover, having a coach or mentor can serve as an accountability partner, ensuring that one remains committed and focused on their PKM goals.

Wrapping up, the journey of PKM, while filled with individual insights and discoveries, can be significantly enriched by leveraging community and external support. By doing so, one not only amplifies their own knowledge journey but also contributes to a larger ecosystem of shared learning and growth.

Reflecting on the Odyssey of Knowledge

As we navigate the vast expanse of personal knowledge management, every step taken, whether it feels significant or minuscule, contributes to a broader tapestry of growth and learning. Overcoming challenges isn't just about reaching the next milestone; it's about the evolution, the metamorphosis that occurs with each hurdle crossed and each obstacle maneuvered around. Each challenge faced and conquered adds another chapter to our story, enriching our experience and imbuing us with deeper insights and understanding.

This journey of PKM, however, is not a linear one. Its beauty lies in its meandering nature, full of twists, turns, and enlightening detours. While the destination might remain elusive, the journey itself offers boundless opportunities for growth and discovery. It's a reminder that in the realm of knowledge, stagnation is not an option. The world of information is dynamic, continuously expanding, and reshaping itself. As such, our approach to managing and harnessing this information must be equally adaptive.

In embracing PKM, we commit to a lifetime of learning, refining, and evolving. It's a voyage that demands resilience, curiosity, and adaptability. But, as with any great odyssey, the rewards are manifold: a sharper mind, a richer perspective, and an ever-expanding horizon of understanding. So, as we move forward, let's celebrate not just the milestones achieved but also the wisdom gained, the connections made, and the myriad ways we've grown along this exhilarating path.

Chapter 10:

PKM for Career Advancement

Introduction: Knowledge as the New Currency in the Career Landscape

In today's rapidly changing job market, where industries are continually being disrupted and the nature of work itself is evolving, knowledge has emerged as a new form of currency. While skills and experience remain essential, the ability to acquire, manage, and apply knowledge has become increasingly important for career advancement. In many ways, the traditional paradigms that have long guided professional success are giving way to a more fluid and complex landscape, one where the mastery of specialized information and the ability to adapt are key drivers of career longevity and success. This shift has made the practice of Personal Knowledge Management (PKM) not just a valuable personal endeavor but also a professional necessity.

The concept of knowledge as currency isn't entirely new, but the degree to which it has become the cornerstone of professional life is unprecedented. Previously, a fixed set of skills and a robust network could guarantee a stable and successful career. Nowadays, while those elements still hold value, they are increasingly insufficient on their own. With the rapid pace of technological development, the spread of globalization, and the increasing complexity of problems that businesses aim to solve, there is a heightened demand for specialized knowledge and the skills to apply it effectively. Whether you're a software engineer needing to keep up with new programming languages, a healthcare professional keeping abreast of the latest treatments, or a marketer navigating the changing algorithms of social media platforms, specialization has become a must.

However, specialization doesn't mean locking oneself into a narrow field without the flexibility to adapt and grow. The modern job market also values versatility—a balanced combination of depth and breadth in your knowledge portfolio. As companies and industries evolve, professionals who can wear multiple hats, who can shift between different roles and functions, are increasingly in demand. Specialization and versatility are not mutually exclusive but are, in fact, complementary facets of a well-rounded professional profile.

This brings us to the importance of PKM in career advancement. PKM is not just a set of techniques for organizing files or a glorified to-do list. It's a comprehensive approach to gathering, curating, synthesizing, and applying information. As you move up the career ladder or switch roles or industries, the body of knowledge you need to master grows and evolves. PKM helps you keep track of this information, ensuring that you are continually learning and that your expertise remains relevant and updated. In essence, it acts as a form of intellectual capital, equipping you with the insights and understanding necessary for making informed decisions, solving complex problems, and, ultimately, adding value to your organization.

Moreover, PKM allows you to leverage your knowledge more effectively. Through organized repositories and frameworks, you can readily access the information you need when you need it. This not only enhances your efficiency but also places you in a position to share your knowledge, making you an invaluable resource to your team and a more attractive candidate for leadership roles. Your capacity to manage and mobilize knowledge influences how you are perceived in your professional community—whether as someone who merely holds a job or as a thought leader who shapes the future of your field.

In summary, as we traverse the complex terrains of the modern career landscape, where knowledge specialization and versatility have gained paramount importance, PKM serves as both an anchor and a sail. It grounds us in the depth of specialized expertise while giving us the wings to adapt and explore the breadth of interdisciplinary understanding. It is a tool for both personal growth and professional leverage, elevating us from mere participants in our respective industries to architects of our own destinies.

Tailoring Your PKM for Specific Career Goals

A one-size-fits-all approach to Personal Knowledge Management (PKM) can only get you so far. To truly maximize its benefits, particularly as it relates to advancing your career, you'll need to customize your PKM strategies based on your unique career objectives. Understanding how to align your knowledge management practices with your goals can give you a distinct advantage in an increasingly competitive professional landscape. Let's delve into several key areas where PKM can be customized to serve your specific career aspirations.

Goal Setting: Establishing Clear and Measurable Career Objectives
Your career goals serve as the North Star that guides all your professional endeavors, including your PKM activities. Goals bring clarity and focus, giving you a framework within which you can allocate your time, energy, and resources more efficiently. A well-defined career objective could be as specific as becoming a project manager in a tech company within two years or as broad as becoming an industry leader in sustainable energy solutions over the next decade. Regardless of the specifics, having clear and measurable objectives allows you to tailor your PKM efforts to be in line with what you hope to achieve professionally.

PKM Alignment: Modifying Knowledge Intake, Synthesis, and Application Based on Career Aspirations
Once your career goals are in place, you can begin to align your PKM activities accordingly. If, for example, you aspire to specialize in cybersecurity, your knowledge intake should involve not only general tech news but also in-depth articles, white papers, and studies specifically related to cybersecurity. Your knowledge synthesis, in turn, could involve creating a dedicated repository of cybersecurity trends, risks, and mitigation strategies, while your application of this knowledge might take the form of targeted projects or even informational content that establishes

your authority in this area. Thus, each facet of your PKM—intake, synthesis, and application—needs to be intentionally focused on serving your career aspirations.

Continuous Learning: Identifying and Pursuing Relevant Certifications, Courses, and Workshops

Continuous learning is a natural extension of PKM, especially when tailored to your career goals. Beyond the informal learning that comes through reading, research, and professional experience, you should also consider more structured forms of learning like certifications, courses, and workshops. These not only enrich your knowledge base but also provide you with the credentials to back up your expertise. Choose learning opportunities that align with your career objectives. If your goal is to transition into data science, for instance, certifications in machine learning or specialized courses in statistical analysis could be highly beneficial.

Networking: Using PKM to Forge Meaningful Professional Connections in Your Desired Field

Your PKM system can be a potent tool for networking. By maintaining a well-organized repository of knowledge, you put yourself in a position to contribute value in discussions, both online and offline. Whether you are engaging with industry leaders on LinkedIn or attending a conference in your field, the ability to recall and share relevant information can help you forge more meaningful connections. Additionally, you can use your PKM system to keep track of your network, noting the expertise and interests of the professionals you meet, so that you can engage with them in a more personalized and impactful manner later on.

With all these considerations, it becomes evident that PKM is not a static or isolated practice but an evolving, integrated component of your broader career strategy. By aligning your PKM system with your career goals, you equip yourself with a dynamic tool set for professional advancement. It enables you to move purposefully through the labyrinth of modern career challenges, turning you into an adaptable, continually learning, and deeply knowledgeable professional.

PKM during Job Transitions and Role Changes

Whether it's by necessity or choice, job transitions and role changes are an inevitable part of today's career landscape. During these periods of change, your Personal Knowledge Management (PKM) system can serve as both a compass and a lifeline. The well-documented and organized knowledge you have gathered can make these transitions smoother and more effective. Here we'll explore how you can leverage PKM to your advantage during these pivotal moments in your career.

The Knowledge Audit: Evaluating Current Knowledge Assets and Identifying Gaps

One of the first steps to take when considering or undergoing a job transition is to conduct a comprehensive knowledge audit. This entails evaluating the current state of your knowledge assets to see what is directly applicable to your new role or field and what is not. Through this self-assessment, you identify gaps that need to be filled for you to be effective in your new position. A knowledge audit can be as simple as a reflective mental inventory or as detailed as a spreadsheet that maps out different knowledge areas, subcategories, and proficiency levels. Armed with this information, you can then devise a targeted learning plan that addresses these gaps, which could be in the form of specialized training, online courses, or mentorship.

Transferable Skills: Recognizing and Presenting Skills that Can Be Applied Across Diverse Roles

A shift in your career trajectory often involves taking on roles that may not be a direct extension of your previous work experience. This is where recognizing and leveraging your transferable skills comes into play. Through your PKM, you can identify and document skills that are not just role-specific but also have broader applicability. For example, if you've honed your project management skills in a tech environment, these can be transferable to a role in healthcare or finance with some adjustments. Your PKM system can help you catalog these skills and keep them at your fingertips, making it easier to articulate your value during interviews or when networking for a role change.

Learning Agility: Rapidly Adapting and Integrating New Knowledge During Transitions

Learning agility is the ability to learn, unlearn, and relearn swiftly, and it is a crucial competency to possess, especially during job transitions. A well-structured PKM system can significantly bolster your learning agility by providing a framework for quick intake, processing, and application of new information. As you integrate into a new role or environment, you can leverage your PKM to organize and assimilate role-specific terminologies, workflows, and best practices. This allows you to get up to speed quicker than you would otherwise, making you an asset to your new team from the get-go.

Embracing Change: Mental Strategies and Practices to Navigate the Uncertainties of Job Shifts

Job transitions can be accompanied by uncertainties, anxieties, and even a sense of loss. Here, PKM isn't just a tool for managing information but also a mental resource. The discipline involved in PKM—from setting clear objectives to establishing daily habits—can be mirrored in how you approach the psychological aspects of a career change. Being systematic about gathering knowledge to navigate your transition can instill a sense of control and purpose, mitigating feelings of uncertainty. Moreover, reflecting on past successes and learning stored within your PKM system can serve as a confidence booster, reinforcing the belief that you have the tools and the acumen to thrive in your new role.

Transitioning between roles or jobs is not merely a procedural change; it's a journey that involves a blend of emotional and intellectual adaptations. As such, your PKM system becomes more than a mere repository of knowledge—it transforms into a dynamic tool for self-assessment, learning, and emotional resilience. It supports you as you cross the bridge from one professional chapter to the next, enabling you to arrive at your new destination not just prepared, but poised for success.

Standing Out in the Professional World with Your Knowledge Portfolio

In a sea of resumes, cover letters, and LinkedIn profiles, what sets you apart from the rest of the talented individuals in your field? One compelling answer to that question lies in the concept of a "knowledge portfolio"—a tangible or digital collection that showcases not just what you've done, but what you know. Your Personal Knowledge Management (PKM) system, when diligently maintained and smartly leveraged, can help you craft an impressive knowledge portfolio that sets you apart in the professional world. Let's explore how to do this in various contexts.

Crafting a Compelling Portfolio: Showcase Projects, Reflections, and Key Learning

A compelling knowledge portfolio goes beyond the traditional resume to provide a deeper look into your expertise and experiences. It includes not just a list of jobs held and projects completed but also reflections on what you've learned, how you've solved problems, and how you've contributed to your team or industry. Your PKM system is a rich source from which to draw this material, as it's where you've been storing, synthesizing, and applying your knowledge. Using it as a foundation, you can craft a portfolio that tells a more complete story about you as a professional, incorporating not just your technical skills but also your thought leadership, ingenuity, and adaptability.

Digital Footprint: Leveraging Platforms Like LinkedIn, Medium, or Personal Blogs to Share Insights and Expertise

In our digital age, your online presence often serves as your first impression. Platforms like LinkedIn, Medium, or personal blogs offer excellent opportunities to demonstrate your professional value. Based on the knowledge you've accumulated and organized through your PKM system, you can produce articles, white papers, or thought pieces that showcase your expertise and perspective. You can share project postmortems that detail how you led a team to success, or technical guides that solve common problems in your field. By consistently sharing high-quality content, you build a digital footprint that not only reflects your skill set but also establishes you as a thought leader in your industry.

Interviews and Negotiations: Utilizing Your PKM to Demonstrate Value and Negotiate Better Terms

When it comes to interviews and negotiations, preparation is key, and this is another area where your PKM system can be invaluable. Because you've meticulously gathered and synthesized knowledge, you can quickly prepare for interviews by reviewing your stored information on industry trends, company background, and role-specific competencies. In negotiations, you can utilize your well-documented skills and accomplishments to make a compelling case for better terms, be it higher compensation, more flexible work arrangements, or expanded responsibilities. Your PKM essentially becomes an evidence-based tool that demonstrates your worth and potential contribution to the organization.

Continuous Updates: Keeping Your Knowledge Portfolio Current in an Ever-evolving Job Market

One crucial aspect often overlooked in maintaining a knowledge portfolio is the need for continuous updates. As the job market evolves, so should your portfolio. This is more than just adding a new project or job role; it's also about updating your reflections, insights, and showcased skills to remain relevant. New certifications, recently acquired skills, or insights from a completed project should be incorporated to keep your portfolio as current as possible. Your PKM system makes this task less daunting by serving as a continually updated repository of your professional self. With each new experience or learning, you update your PKM system, and consequently, it becomes a relatively simple matter to keep your public knowledge portfolio in step with your evolving career.

Through these multifaceted approaches, your PKM system becomes the backbone of a dynamic, compelling knowledge portfolio—one that serves as a vivid testament to your abilities, achievements, and potential. It's a portfolio that doesn't just answer the question of what you've done but goes much further to explain who you are as a professional, what you bring to the table, and how you adapt and grow. In an age where everyone is looking for an edge, a meticulously crafted and maintained knowledge portfolio could very well be the key that unlocks your next big opportunity.

Mentorship, Leadership, and PKM

The trajectory of professional success isn't a solitary journey; it often intersects with roles that involve guiding others and taking on leadership responsibilities. In this context, your Personal Knowledge Management (PKM) system can be a significant asset, not just for your individual growth but also in your interactions with peers, mente's, and even superiors. Here's how a robust PKM system can elevate you into leadership roles, assist in mentoring, and help establish credibility and trust within your professional network.

Role of PKM in Ascending to Leadership Positions
Leadership is as much about guiding others as it is about possessing the necessary technical or operational skills to do a job. Effective leaders are reservoirs of knowledge; they are expected to have an overview of their domain and an understanding of how various pieces fit together. As you rise through the ranks, the scope of what you need to know expands. A well-structured PKM system allows you to keep track of this increasingly complex and broad body of knowledge, making it easier for you to adapt to the demands of higher-level roles.

Moreover, as a leader, decision-making is a crucial part of your responsibilities. Your PKM system can be invaluable in this regard, serving as a repository of case studies, best practices, and lessons learned from both successes and failures. This wealth of organized information can guide you in making informed decisions, positioning you as someone who is thoughtful, prepared, and capable—a leader in the truest sense.

How a Well-Maintained PKM System Can Aid in Mentoring and Guiding Others
In a mentorship role, you're expected to provide guidance, insights, and actionable advice. A comprehensive PKM system gives you a unique advantage, as it acts like an extended brain where you've stored not only technical information but also your thoughts on soft skills like

communication, problem-solving, and team dynamics. With such a wealth of information at your fingertips, you're better equipped to provide valuable guidance tailored to different situations and individual needs.

Furthermore, your PKM system can serve as a teaching tool. Imagine being able to quickly access a relevant article, study, or personal reflection that can aid in illustrating a point or resolving a query. In doing so, you not only answer a mente's question but also teach them how to fish for information themselves, setting them up for long-term success.

Sharing Knowledge as a Means of Establishing Credibility and Trust in Professional Circles

The saying "Knowledge is power" holds particular relevance in the professional world. However, the true power of knowledge doesn't just lie in acquiring it, but also in sharing it effectively. Your PKM system can be an essential tool for knowledge dissemination. Whether it's by contributing to internal wikis, leading workshops, or speaking at industry conferences, sharing valuable insights can position you as a trusted authority in your field.

This kind of credibility is not merely beneficial for personal branding; it also fosters trust among colleagues and superiors. When people realize you're not just hoarding knowledge for personal gain but are willing to share it to uplift the team or contribute to broader organizational goals, it greatly enhances your reputation. You're seen not just as a repository of information but as a resourceful, reliable, and cooperative member of the community.

So, as you consider your professional journey, understand that PKM isn't a solitary endeavor; it's a communal one. Your individual success, fueled by a well-managed body of knowledge, contributes to collective achievements, whether you're guiding a mentee, leading a team, or contributing to your professional community. In doing so, you're not just climbing your career ladder; you're also laying down the rungs for others to ascend alongside you.

Navigating Career Challenges with PKM

No professional journey is devoid of bumps, detours, or roadblocks. Setbacks, whether minor or major, are an inevitable part of any career path. However, how you navigate these challenges can significantly impact your professional growth and personal well-being. This is where your Personal Knowledge Management (PKM) system can prove invaluable, serving as a strategic asset that enables you to approach career challenges with resilience, versatility, and ingenuity.

Using Your PKM as a Fallback During Career Setbacks
Life is unpredictable, and sometimes despite your best efforts, setbacks such as job loss, demotion, or unsuccessful projects can occur. In times like these, your PKM serves as a powerful fallback resource. Within its organized structure, you have a detailed account of your skills, accomplishments, learnings, and even your professional network. This provides you with a firm foundation from which to reassess, recalibrate, and relaunch your career. Your PKM system can help you take stock of your strengths and areas for improvement, thereby enabling you to plot a more focused and informed path forward.

Leveraging Your Knowledge Assets to Diversify Career Paths or Start Entrepreneurial Ventures
A well-curated PKM system can be likened to a diverse investment portfolio, offering you options to pivot or diversify your career when necessary. For instance, the cumulative knowledge and skills you've gathered can open doors to alternative career paths that you may not have initially considered. Perhaps you've acquired a wealth of information on sustainable practices within your industry; this could pave the way for consultancy work or even starting an entrepreneurial venture in sustainability. Your PKM, therefore, equips you with the necessary assets to diversify your professional path, whether that means venturing into new sectors, freelance consulting, or even starting your own business.

PKM as a Tool for Resilience and Reinvention in the Face of Professional Adversity

The most significant benefit of having a robust PKM system during challenging times is perhaps its role in fostering resilience and enabling reinvention. Resilience is not merely about enduring difficulties but adapting and growing in the face of them. Your PKM is a tool that aids in this transformative process. With all your professional experiences and acquired knowledge neatly organized, you can more readily see patterns, identify gaps, and assess opportunities for growth.

Imagine facing a career crisis where you're questioning your professional identity or worth. Your PKM serves as a tangible reminder of your competencies, achievements, and contributions, providing the psychological boost to face adversities with a clearer mind. Furthermore, your PKM isn't a static entity but a continuously evolving system that you can adapt to your changing circumstances. This dynamic nature of PKM makes it a tool for reinvention. As you navigate through professional adversity, you can add to it new learnings, skills, and experiences that not only help you overcome current challenges but also better equip you for future ones.

Navigating through the winding and often treacherous road of professional life requires more than just technical prowess or strategic acumen; it demands resilience, versatility, and the continuous ability to learn and adapt. Your PKM system is an ally in this journey, offering you a structured way to manage the ever-complex tapestry of skills, knowledge, and experiences that define your career. Whether you're bouncing back from setbacks, diversifying your career options, or reimagining your professional self, PKM provides the framework to do it with greater confidence and efficacy.

Future proofing Your Career with PKM

In a world where technological advancements, market dynamics, and global events can radically shift the job landscape, the notion of a "secure job" has become more of a relic than a reality. Today's professionals need to look beyond merely excelling in their current roles and consider how to future-proof their careers against uncertainties and disruptions. Personal Knowledge Management (PKM) can be a central element of this strategy, allowing you to proactively navigate the shifting currents of the professional world. Here's how a robust PKM system can help you ensure career longevity and adaptability.

Staying Ahead of Industry Trends and Changes Through Vigilant Knowledge Management

Change is the only constant, especially in the professional realm. Industries are evolving at breakneck speeds due to technological innovations, regulatory shifts, and consumer behaviors, among other factors. With a vigilant approach to knowledge management, you can stay ahead of these changes rather than being swept away by them. Your PKM system can be geared to continuously monitor, analyze, and assimilate industry trends, technological advancements, and emerging best practices. By routinely updating this information and cross-referencing it with your existing knowledge base, you equip yourself with the insights needed to not just survive but thrive amidst change. You become one of the few who can anticipate trends rather than merely react to them, making you an invaluable asset to any organization.

Lifelong Learning as a Strategy for Career Longevity

One of the fundamental tenets of PKM is the commitment to continuous learning. As you progress in your career, the focus often shifts from learning to doing, with many falling into the complacency of believing they "know enough." However, in a world marked by constant upheaval and change, lifelong learning isn't a luxury; it's a necessity for career longevity.

Your PKM system serves as both a repository and a roadmap for this lifelong learning journey. It is where you store what you've learned, yes, but it's also where you identify gaps, set new learning objectives, and chart courses of study or exploration. Whether it's taking up new courses, attending webinars, or even going back to school, your PKM aids you in making these decisions with a clear understanding of how they align with your long-term career objectives and the evolving demands of your industry.

Adapting to the Evolving Demands of the Future Job Market with a Robust PKM System

The future job market won't just demand new skills; it will demand new ways of thinking and problem-solving. Soft skills like adaptability, critical thinking, and emotional intelligence are increasingly becoming as important as technical proficiency. A well-maintained PKM system isn't just a catalog of what you know but a framework for how you think. By practicing the conscious organization, synthesis, and application of knowledge, you're also honing your ability to assimilate new information, make connections, and adapt to new situations. This mental nimbleness will be one of your greatest assets as you navigate the evolving demands of the future job market.

In conclusion, the future may be uncertain, but that doesn't mean you can't prepare for it. Through vigilant knowledge management, a commitment to lifelong learning, and the development of both hard and soft skills, your PKM system can serve as a powerful tool for future-proofing your career. It can transform you from a passive participant in your career journey into an active navigator, capable of steering through the uncertainties and opportunities that the future inevitably holds.

As we come to the close of this exploration into the intricate relationship between career advancement and Personal Knowledge Management (PKM), a few key insights emerge that warrant reflection. The first is the almost symbiotic relationship between career growth and effective PKM. Far from being separate entities, they feed into each other in a cycle of perpetual improvement. A strong PKM system not only propels your career forward but also evolves and enriches itself as your career progresses, creating a loop of continual growth and refinement.

Understanding and leveraging this symbiosis can unlock new dimensions in your professional life. It allows you to stay ahead of industry changes, diversify your skill set, provide mentorship, build your professional reputation, and even bounce back from setbacks with greater resilience. It becomes a tool for navigation in the uncharted waters of your career, serving as both compass and anchor.

That leads us to the final, perhaps the most crucial point: a call to action. The power of PKM as a cornerstone of your professional journey becomes truly significant when it's a constant endeavor. It isn't a one-time setup but a lifelong commitment to learning, organizing, and applying knowledge. Whether you're at the beginning of your career, facing a transitional moment, or even looking to give back through mentorship, investing in your PKM system will yield dividends that go beyond the professional sphere into personal fulfillment and lifelong learning.

Therefore, as you continue on your professional path, consider your PKM system as not just a repository but as a living, evolving partner in your journey. Make the commitment today to invest in it continuously, update it meticulously, and consult it regularly. In doing so, you lay the groundwork for a career marked not just by success, but by significance and fulfillment.

Chapter 11

PKM for Entrepreneurs

The Entrepreneurial Edge in a Knowledge Driven World

In the contemporary landscape of business, characterized by digital technologies, fast-paced innovation, and global markets, entrepreneurs face a unique set of challenges and opportunities. While the barriers to entry have been significantly lowered—thanks to technology—competition has also intensified, with markets becoming more crowded and consumers more discerning. Navigating this dynamic and often volatile environment requires more than just a good product or service. Entrepreneurs need to be agile learners, adept problem-solvers, and, above all, effective managers of information and knowledge. In this context, Personal Knowledge Management (PKM) emerges not just as a useful tool but as a secret weapon for entrepreneurial success.

Being an entrepreneur in the digital age comes with its own set of peculiar challenges. The speed at which industries are evolving demands constant vigilance and adaptability. Moreover, the sheer volume of information and resources available can be overwhelming. Entrepreneurs have to wear multiple hats, shifting seamlessly from product development to marketing, from finance to human resources. Each of these roles requires specialized knowledge, and keeping up with best practices and innovations in even one area can be a daunting task.

However, where challenges abound, opportunities also flourish. The same digital tools and platforms that inundate us with information also provide unparalleled access to resources, learning materials, and even global markets. With the right strategies, small startups can compete with well-established firms, reaching customers and scaling operations in ways that were unthinkable just a few years ago. Here is where PKM plays a transformative role.

PKM allows entrepreneurs to systematize the often chaotic process of information gathering, organization, and application. When you're running a startup or a small business, time is your most limited resource. A well-implemented PKM system streamlines your workflow by ensuring that the right information is available at the right time, allowing for faster decision-making and problem-solving. It can help you stay abreast of industry trends, monitor competitor strategies, and continually update your own skills and knowledge. Essentially, PKM amplifies your capacity to learn and adapt, which are fundamental traits for entrepreneurial success.

But PKM's utility goes beyond mere personal organization. As your venture grows, PKM can evolve into a broader knowledge management system that permeates your organization. It can assist in training and onboarding employees, establishing a culture of continuous learning, and even play a role in customer engagement strategies. In short, PKM isn't just a tool for personal efficiency; it has the potential to become a foundational element of your business strategy.

Therefore, as we delve into the many facets of using PKM for entrepreneurial endeavors, think of it as an investment not just in your individual capability but in the long-term resilience and competitiveness of your venture. It's an investment in cultivating a systematic approach to knowledge that could very well become your entrepreneurial edge in a knowledge-driven world.

Harnessing PKM for Market Research and Trend Analysis

When venturing into the entrepreneurial world, staying attuned to market dynamics is paramount. One misstep or missed opportunity can be the difference between success and failure. Market research and trend analysis are the cornerstones of informed decision-making, and here, Personal Knowledge Management (PKM) can act as a catalyst, streamlining the process and amplifying the insights gained. Let's explore how PKM can be harnessed for this critical aspect of entrepreneurship.

The Importance of Informed Decision Making: Using Data and Knowledge as the Backbone of Entrepreneurial Choices

Every entrepreneur faces a myriad of decisions, ranging from product development nuances to marketing strategies and pricing models. The quality of these decisions often determines the trajectory of the venture. Making choices based on gut feeling or anecdotal evidence might sometimes work, but it's akin to gambling. A more reliable strategy is to base decisions on well-researched information and actionable insights. This is where your PKM system comes into play. By continually gathering and organizing relevant data and knowledge, you establish a robust backbone for your entrepreneurial choices. Over time, your PKM system becomes a rich resource that you can tap into whenever you need to make a decision, thereby significantly reducing risk and improving the likelihood of success.

Tools and Techniques: Platforms and Methodologies for Comprehensive Market Research

Conducting market research is often seen as a cumbersome process, but it doesn't have to be. Several digital tools and platforms can assist in gathering valuable market insights, from Google Trends and SEMrush for search behavior to platforms like SurveyMonkey for customer surveys. Within your PKM system, you can set up specific folders or tags for market research, where you collect, categorize, and annotate information. This organized repository can include customer feedback, competitor analysis, industry reports, and more. The PKM system can also help you keep track of the methodologies you've found most effective, offering a dual advantage: a body of market-related knowledge and a methodology for how to update and expand it.

Trend Spotting: Identifying and Analyzing Emerging Market Trends Using a PKM Approach

In the fast-paced entrepreneurial world, the early bird often does catch the worm. Being among the first to identify an emerging market trend can give you a significant competitive advantage. Your PKM system can be invaluable for this kind of trend spotting. By keeping tabs on a range of sources, from industry publications to influential social media accounts, and systematically capturing and analyzing this information, you can often identify patterns and trends before they become obvious to the broader market. Within your PKM system, you can create a dedicated space for potential trends, where you aggregate related data points, news items, and personal observations, allowing for a more in-depth analysis to assess the potential impact and opportunities associated with each trend.

Validating Ideas: Cross-referencing Concepts with Gathered Knowledge to Test Viability

One of the most exhilarating aspects of entrepreneurship is the process of idea generation. However, not all bright ideas are necessarily good business opportunities. The challenge lies in filtering through these sparks of inspiration to find those worth pursuing. Your PKM system can aid significantly in this validation process. By cross-referencing your new ideas with the data and insights already stored in your PKM, you can quickly assess their viability. For example, you might have a product feature idea that you think is groundbreaking. By consulting your PKM system, you can check if similar features have been tried before, how they were received by customers, and what challenges they faced. This method allows you to quickly weed out ideas that are less likely to succeed, enabling you to focus your energy and resources on the most promising opportunities.

So, as you navigate the complex terrain of entrepreneurship, consider your PKM system as more than just a personal database. View it as an intelligent interface for market research and analysis, a tool that sharpens your decision-making and enables you to stay ahead of the curve. It equips you with the insights to not just exist in the market but to understand it deeply, anticipate its movements, and act with strategic precision.

Organizing Business Ideas, Pitches, and Strategies

Entrepreneurship is an art form that thrives on creativity, spontaneity, and inspiration. Yet, like any art, its impact is significantly magnified when infused with structure and precision. This balance between inspiration and structure is where Personal Knowledge Management (PKM) can offer entrepreneurs an undeniable advantage. By organizing business ideas, fine-tuning pitches, and facilitating strategic planning, PKM becomes the underpinning architecture for entrepreneurial success.

Idea Repository: Creating a Structured System to Capture and Refine Business Ideas

The entrepreneurial journey often starts with a simple idea, but these ideas are notoriously fleeting. Having a structured repository within your PKM system can ensure that these sparks of creativity are not just captured but also refined over time. Create a specific section dedicated to business ideas, where each idea is given its dedicated space for expansion, analysis, and scrutiny. As you come across relevant articles, market data, or competitor information, you can append these to the corresponding idea, allowing for a more nuanced understanding of its potential and feasibility. Over time, this repository becomes a goldmine for entrepreneurial ventures, providing you with a well-organized list of business ideas, each supported by a wealth of contextual information and insights.

Pitch Preparation: Utilizing PKM to Craft Compelling Presentations for Investors and Stakeholders

Pitching to investors or stakeholders is a pivotal moment for any entrepreneur. While the quality of your idea undoubtedly matters, the effectiveness of your presentation can be equally crucial. Your PKM system can serve as a valuable resource in this regard, helping you to craft pitches that are not just compelling but also deeply informed. Within your PKM, you can maintain a section dedicated to pitch preparation, containing successful pitch examples, tips on public speaking, crucial questions often raised by investors, and the like. As you prepare for a pitch, you can draw upon these resources to shape your presentation, ensuring it addresses the concerns that are top of mind for your audience. This approach significantly heightens your chances of not just capturing their attention but also securing their buy-in.

Strategic Planning: Integrating Knowledge Assets into Actionable Business Strategies

Strategic planning is where the rubber meets the road in entrepreneurship. At this stage, ideas must be transformed into actionable plans, guided by both short-term goals and long-term vision. Your PKM system can play an instrumental role here by integrating various knowledge assets into a coherent strategy. From market trends and consumer behavior to competitor strategies and operational best practices, your PKM system houses a broad spectrum of information. Strategic planning can be significantly enhanced by leveraging this organized knowledge to create business plans that are both ambitious and grounded in reality. For instance, your market research can directly inform your go-to-market strategy, while insights on consumer behavior can shape your customer engagement initiatives.

Monitoring and Adapting: Using PKM to Track Business Performance and Make Informed Tweaks

Entrepreneurial ventures are living entities that need constant monitoring and occasional tweaking to align with market dynamics. Here, too, PKM proves invaluable. By maintaining a section dedicated to performance metrics, market feedback, and other key indicators, you can create a real-time dashboard of sorts within your PKM system. Regularly update this section with new data and observations, allowing you to track how your business is performing against your strategic objectives. Should deviations occur, you can refer back to your rich pool of knowledge to understand the possible causes and adapt your strategies accordingly. This dynamic use of PKM turns it into an agile tool that helps you stay responsive to market realities.

As you build and evolve your entrepreneurial venture, the role of PKM expands from being a mere filing system to an active business partner. It becomes your go-to hub for ideas, your preparation ground for important pitches, your strategic think-tank for planning, and your control room for monitoring and adaptation. By integrating PKM into these various facets of entrepreneurship, you're not just organizing your business activities;

you're supercharging them, setting the stage for a venture that's both agile and robust.

Networking and Building Partnerships through Effective Knowledge Sharing

Entrepreneurial success is often a collective endeavor, influenced by the networks you create, the partnerships you forge, and the collaborations you engage in. In this social dimension of entrepreneurship, Personal Knowledge Management (PKM) can be an incredibly potent tool. It can help you elevate your interactions, share your expertise, and build trust within your professional circle. Let's explore how PKM can enhance networking and partnership-building activities in entrepreneurial contexts.

Elevating Conversations: Using Your Knowledge Base to Engage in Deeper, Value-Driven Interactions
Networking events and business meetings frequently feature surface-level discussions that seldom go beyond introductions and business card exchanges. However, the most fruitful relationships often stem from conversations that dig deeper, offering both parties genuine value. Armed with a well-curated PKM system, you're equipped to elevate conversations from mere pleasantries to more meaningful, value-driven interactions. You can effortlessly bring in relevant data points, industry insights, or emerging trends that could benefit your interlocutor. By doing so, you position yourself as someone who brings tangible value to the relationship, thereby increasing the likelihood of ongoing engagement and potential collaboration.

Collaboration Platforms: Tools for Collaborative Knowledge Management in Entrepreneurial Settings
In an increasingly digital world, entrepreneurs often work with remote teams, freelancers, and partners spread across geographies. This dispersed work environment requires robust collaborative tools, and your PKM strategy should be adaptable to this reality. There are numerous platforms available that facilitate collaborative knowledge management, such as Microsoft Teams, Slack, or Asana. Within these platforms, you can create

dedicated channels or boards that serve as communal PKM spaces, where team members can share valuable articles, project updates, and other relevant resources. By taking your PKM system beyond the individual and into the collective, you lay the groundwork for a culture of knowledge sharing and collective growth within your entrepreneurial venture.

Building Trust: Demonstrating Expertise and Reliability Through Consistent Knowledge Sharing

In any professional relationship, trust is a valuable currency. One of the most effective ways to build trust is through consistent knowledge sharing. When you consistently offer valuable insights, advice, or resources, you demonstrate not just your expertise but also your reliability and willingness to contribute to mutual success. Your PKM system facilitates this by serving as a repository from which you can regularly draw valuable content to share with your network. Whether it's sending a recent industry report to a potential investor or sharing a useful tool with a fellow entrepreneur, the act of sharing not only enriches the recipient but also fortifies your reputation as a reliable and knowledgeable player in your field.

Networking Strategies: Leveraging Conferences, Seminars, and Online Platforms to Expand Business Connections Using PKM

The networking landscape offers a variety of platforms, from traditional conferences and seminars to online webinars and social media platforms like LinkedIn. A strategic approach to networking involves leveraging these various avenues in a manner that aligns with your entrepreneurial goals. Your PKM can aid in this by helping you prepare for different networking scenarios. For instance, if you're attending an industry conference, your PKM system can provide you with the latest trends and talking points to engage in informed discussions. Similarly, on platforms like LinkedIn, you can use your PKM to regularly share valuable content, thereby attracting a wider yet targeted professional audience.

In essence, your PKM system serves as the bedrock upon which you can build a rich tapestry of professional relationships and collaborations. By enabling you to engage in more meaningful conversations, collaborate more efficiently, build trust through knowledge sharing, and network more strategically, PKM transforms the social dimensions of entrepreneurship from a game of chance to a well-orchestrated strategy. It's this strategic approach to networking and partnerships that often marks the difference between entrepreneurial ventures that merely survive and those that truly thrive.

Knowledge-Driven Product Development and Service Design

In the competitive landscape of entrepreneurship, a static product or service is often a recipe for stagnation or decline. Continuous iteration, fueled by user feedback, market intelligence, and technological advancements, is essential for long-term success. Personal Knowledge Management (PKM) plays a pivotal role in making this iterative process more structured, informed, and effective. Let's delve into how a knowledge-driven approach can significantly impact your product development and service design.

Implementing User Feedback and Market Knowledge into Product/Service Iterations

Understanding user needs and expectations is at the core of any successful product or service. However, capturing this feedback is just the first step; the real challenge lies in effectively incorporating it into your product or service offerings. A well-maintained PKM system can serve as the ideal platform for aggregating user feedback, organizing it by themes or features, and linking it to actionable items in your development cycle. In the same vein, your PKM can house vital market intelligence—such as competitor offerings or industry benchmarks—that can offer additional context to user feedback. By synthesizing these multiple layers of information, you enable more nuanced iterations that are both user-centric and market-aware, thereby enhancing your chances of delivering a product or service that resonates with your target audience.

Utilizing PKM to Stay Updated with Technological Advancements and Integration Possibilities

The pace at which technology is advancing offers both challenges and opportunities for entrepreneurs. On the one hand, it's easy to get overwhelmed or even outpaced by these advancements. On the other hand, these technologies often open up new avenues for product or service innovation. Here, PKM becomes a vital tool for staying abreast of relevant technological trends. You can create specific categories or tags within your PKM system for emerging technologies that could be integrated into your product or service. This repository becomes a point of reference that you can consult regularly, ensuring that you are not only aware of new technologies but also well-positioned to implement them into your offerings as appropriate.

Design Thinking and PKM: A Synergy for Innovative Solutions
Design thinking is a methodology used for solving complex problems in a user concentric way, and it has found significant resonance in the entrepreneurial world for its effectiveness in product development and service design. PKM and design thinking can work in synergy to create truly innovative solutions. The design thinking process involves stages like empathizing with the user, defining problems, ideating solutions, prototyping, and testing. Each of these stages can be enriched through your PKM system. For instance, the empathize stage might be supported by user interviews and feedback stored in your PKM, while the ideate stage can draw upon the various creative ideas or inspiration snippets you've saved over time. This integration of PKM into your design thinking process ensures that each stage is not only creatively robust but also deeply informed, leading to solutions that are both innovative and viable.

In the final analysis, product development and service design are not standalone activities but ongoing processes deeply intertwined with various facets of entrepreneurship—from user engagement and market dynamics to technological trends. By integrating a knowledge-driven approach through PKM, you ensure that these processes are not conducted in isolation but are contextual, dynamic, and continually refined. This approach elevates your product or service from being a static offering to a continually evolving entity that adapts and grows in harmony with your users' needs and market opportunities. It's this adaptive capacity, fueled by effective knowledge management, that often sets truly successful entrepreneurial ventures apart from the rest.

Funding and Investment: A PKM Approach

Securing funding and managing investments are among the most critical and challenging aspects of entrepreneurship. The stakes are high, and the competition for investor attention is fierce. It's an arena where a data-driven, knowledge concentric approach can be a distinct advantage, offering you a more nuanced understanding of what investors seek and how to appeal to them. Personal Knowledge Management (PKM) can be your strategic asset in this context. Here's how a PKM approach can offer valuable support in navigating the complex world of funding and investment.

Researching Potential Investors and Tailoring Pitches Using a Knowledge Centrist Approach

The process of seeking investment often starts with identifying potential investors who align with your venture's industry, stage, and vision. A rudimentary Google search can yield names, but for a deeper and more nuanced understanding, a PKM approach is beneficial. Within your PKM system, you can maintain a dedicated section where you collate detailed profiles of potential investors, capturing not just their investment history but also their stated interests, sector focus, and even investment philosophies. As you prepare to reach out to them or tailor your investment pitches, this collated knowledge enables you to speak directly to their specific interests and concerns, thereby increasing your pitch's effectiveness and resonance.

Monitoring Financial Trends and Insights to Make Informed Funding Decisions

The financial landscape is a constantly shifting terrain influenced by a myriad of factors, ranging from economic indicators to geopolitical events.

Making informed funding decisions—such as when to seek investment, what valuation to aim for, or which type of funding to pursue—requires a keen understanding of these dynamics. Your PKM system can serve as a real-time dashboard for such financial insights. By systematically gathering and updating information on market valuations, interest rates, investor sentiment, and other relevant financial trends, you create a robust knowledge base. This base can guide your funding decisions, ensuring they are not just instinct-driven but backed by comprehensive data and nuanced analysis.

Preparing for Investor Queries and Discussions with a Robust PKM System

Once you've caught an investor's attention, the next phase involves detailed discussions, queries, and perhaps even negotiations. This stage is often as crucial as the initial pitch, as investors dig deeper into your business model, market viability, and growth plans. A well-structured PKM system can be an invaluable asset in preparing for these discussions. Since you've already been collecting market research, user feedback, competitor analysis, and financial trends within your PKM, you're well-equipped to answer most investor queries with data-backed responses. Additionally, your PKM can also contain potential questions that investors are likely to ask, along with well-thought-out answers. Being prepared in this way not only boosts your confidence but also enhances your credibility in the eyes of potential investors.

The process of securing funding and managing investments is undeniably stressful and complex. However, it's also an area where thorough research, data-driven insights, and meticulous preparation can significantly tip the scales in your favor. By integrating Personal Knowledge Management into your funding and investment strategies, you bring a level of sophistication and readiness that can set you apart in the highly competitive entrepreneurial landscape. Your PKM system becomes more than just a repository of information; it transforms into a strategic tool, empowering you to navigate the intricate dynamics of entrepreneurial finance with greater confidence and efficacy.

Managing Business Risks with PKM

Every entrepreneurial venture carries an inherent level of risk, be it market volatility, competitive pressures, or operational challenges. However, risk should not be equated with gamble. While the former is an inevitable aspect of business, the latter signifies a reliance on chance rather than strategy. Effective risk management is about identifying, understanding, and making calculated decisions to mitigate these risks. In this endeavor, Personal Knowledge Management (PKM) can serve as both a shield and a compass, guiding you through uncertain terrains with a measure of confidence and foresight. Here's how PKM can be a critical tool for managing business risks.

Anticipating Challenges Using a Proactive Knowledge Management Approach

They say forewarned is forearmed. In the world of entrepreneurship, the ability to anticipate challenges often provides a critical advantage. By proactively managing knowledge, you're better equipped to foresee potential pitfalls and challenges. For example, if you're venturing into a highly regulated industry, your PKM system can contain constantly updated information on relevant laws and regulations, thereby enabling you to anticipate compliance challenges. Likewise, by keeping tabs on market trends, consumer behavior, and competitive actions, you can anticipate shifts in the market landscape that may necessitate adjustments in your business strategy. Such a proactive approach not only enhances your readiness but also provides the time needed for devising effective counter-strategies.

Case Studies: Successful Entrepreneurial Decisions Backed by Solid PKM Practices

Learning from the experiences of others can offer valuable insights, especially when it comes to risk management. Incorporating case studies into your PKM system can provide you with real-world examples of both challenges faced and strategies employed by other entrepreneurs. Whether it's a case study about a startup that pivoted effectively in response to market changes or an analysis of a business that failed due to certain operational missteps, each story serves as a learning opportunity. By analyzing these case studies within the context of your own venture, you're not merely learning from others' experiences but also adapting these lessons to your unique circumstances. This application of learned knowledge significantly bolsters your risk management efforts, grounding them in tried and tested realities.

Mitigating Potential Pitfalls by Leveraging the Collective Knowledge of Mentors, Peers, and Industry Leaders

While your PKM system is a powerful tool for personal learning, it can also serve as a conduit for tapping into the collective wisdom of mentors, peers, and industry leaders. You can extend your knowledge management practices to include insights gleaned from networking events, masterclasses, or mentorship sessions. By doing so, you're not just relying on your own understanding but enriching it with the perspectives of those who've navigated similar entrepreneurial journeys. This collective wisdom can be particularly useful in identifying potential risks and blind spots that you may not have considered. When such knowledge is systematically integrated into your PKM system, it serves as an additional layer of armor, offering you broader and deeper insights for risk mitigation.

Risk is an integral part of the entrepreneurial journey, but its negative impact can be substantially minimized through effective management. By integrating Personal Knowledge Management into your risk mitigation strategies, you're arming yourself with a potent blend of foresight, learning, and collective wisdom. This enriched understanding equips you to navigate through the inevitable ups and downs of entrepreneurship, not with trepidation, but with calculated confidence. It turns your PKM system from a mere organizational tool into a strategic asset, one that enables you to face risks not as roadblocks but as challenges to be understood, managed, and ultimately overcome.

As we close this chapter, it becomes unmistakably clear that a robust Personal Knowledge Management (PKM) system is far more than just an organizational convenience; it's a strategic asset that can significantly amplify the chances of entrepreneurial success. From the initial stages of idealization and market research to the complexities of risk management and investor relations, PKM acts as your informational compass. It helps you navigate each step of your entrepreneurial journey, ensuring that your decisions are not made in a vacuum but are supported by a carefully curated body of knowledge. In essence, PKM provides you with an undeniable edge—a form of intellectual capital that can set you apart in the highly competitive entrepreneurial landscape.

However, the potency of PKM lies not just in its initial setup but in its ongoing refinement. The world of entrepreneurship is anything but static. Market dynamics shift, consumer preferences evolve, and technological innovations continually reshape the playing field. In the face of such dynamism, a static PKM system would quickly become obsolete. Therefore, the call to action here is clear: Make your PKM practice a living, evolving entity. Continuously update it with new insights, regularly review its structure to ensure it aligns with your changing business needs, and consciously make it a part of your daily entrepreneurial life.

By committing to this continuous refinement, you're not just keeping your PKM system up-to-date; you're also ensuring that your entrepreneurial decisions are consistently informed, insightful, and adaptive. In a world where information is abundant but wisdom is scarce, a well-maintained PKM system can be your gateway to the latter. So, as you continue on your entrepreneurial journey, view your PKM not just as a repository of what you know, but as a reflection of how you think, learn, and adapt. It's this commitment to continuous learning and adaptation that often delineates the truly successful entrepreneurs from the rest. Take the pledge today to make PKM an integral part of your entrepreneurial strategy, and you'll be investing in a future marked not just by survival but by meaningful success and growth.

Conclusion

Revisiting the PKM Odyssey

As we draw the curtains on this comprehensive exploration of Personal Knowledge Management (PKM), it's both fitting and enriching to pause and reflect on the ground we've covered. This odyssey through the realms of PKM has not merely been an academic exercise; rather, it has served as a practical guide for leveraging the power of knowledge in an era marked by overwhelming information and rapid change. We've witnessed how PKM isn't just a modern luxury but an essential skill set for anyone seeking to thrive in the digital age. It serves as a navigational tool that helps us sift through the deluge of data, identify what's meaningful, and apply it in ways that create tangible impact.

But the story of PKM doesn't end with merely curating and organizing information. Its true strength lies in its transformative potential—its ability to convert raw data into actionable insights and, ultimately, into a form of wisdom that can significantly impact various spheres of life. From personal growth to professional development, from academic pursuits to entrepreneurial ventures, we've seen how a robust PKM system can serve as a catalyst for positive change and meaningful success.

So, as we revisit the PKM odyssey, the journey we've collectively undertaken through these pages, let's appreciate the weight and worth of what we've learned. Let's take a moment to marvel at how structured knowledge is not just an academic or professional asset but a life-enhancing tool that adds layers of depth, understanding, and efficacy to our actions and decisions. It's this transformative power of PKM that elevates it from a methodical practice to a philosophical approach to life—one that empowers us to live not just reactively, but proactively, guided by the richness of curated knowledge and the wisdom it imparts.

The Future of PKM and its Evolving Role in the Business World

As we ponder the path forward for Personal Knowledge Management, it's essential to recognize that the field itself is in a state of continuous evolution, reflective of the larger technological and societal changes sweeping across our world. The PKM systems of tomorrow may bear little resemblance to those of today, both in their capabilities and their impact. As we step into this promising yet uncertain future, several trends and developments stand out as potential game-changers for PKM, particularly within the business landscape.

Predictive Analyses: How Advancements in AI and Machine Learning Might Augment PKM Practices

Artificial Intelligence (AI) and machine learning are set to dramatically impact almost every facet of our lives, and PKM is no exception. Imagine a PKM system that not only helps you organize your current knowledge but also predicts what information you will need in the future. Through predictive analytics, future PKM systems could anticipate market changes, identify upcoming trends, or even suggest areas for personal or professional development. These predictive capabilities could significantly augment our decision-making prowess, ensuring that we're not just reacting to the present but proactively preparing for the future.

Integration with Emerging Technologies: The Role of Virtual Reality, Augmented Reality, and the Metaverse in Shaping Future PKM Tools

The burgeoning fields of Virtual Reality (VR), Augmented Reality (AR), and the broader concept of the Metaverse are opening up entirely new possibilities for how we interact with information. Future PKM systems could leverage these technologies to create more immersive learning and knowledge management experiences. Imagine "walking" through a virtual library of your curated resources, or holding a virtual meeting with your team where actionable insights are presented as interactive holograms. The integration of PKM with these advanced technologies could fundamentally change the way we think about storing, accessing, and applying knowledge.

The Shift to Collective Intelligence: Exploring the Potential of Communal and Shared Knowledge Systems in Businesses and Organizations

While PKM traditionally focuses on individual knowledge management, the concept of collective intelligence is gaining traction. In an increasingly interconnected world, the wisdom of a community often surpasses that of a single individual. Businesses and organizations are exploring systems that enable communal knowledge sharing and decision-making. Future PKM tools could facilitate this shift by offering features that allow for collaborative knowledge curation, consensus-building, and even decentralized decision-making. The notion of PKM could thus expand to encompass not just the individual but also the collective, enhancing both personal productivity and communal outcomes.

Continuous Evolution: Adapting PKM Practices in Response to Rapid Technological and Societal Changes

The only constant is change, and this adage holds particularly true for the technology-infused world we live in. PKM practices will need to continuously evolve to remain effective and relevant. Whether it's adapting to new data privacy regulations, integrating with the latest apps and platforms, or simply updating our approaches to keep pace with our evolving life goals, the future of PKM lies in its adaptability. To make the most of PKM in the coming years, a mindset of perpetual learning and flexibility will be invaluable.

As we stand at the cusp of these exciting advancements and shifts, the role of PKM in our personal and professional lives is poised for a transformative leap. What started as a practice focused on handling information overload is morphing into a sophisticated discipline that can harness the power of technology, community, and foresight. As we adapt to and integrate these burgeoning capabilities, our relationship with knowledge itself is bound to evolve, making the journey of PKM a continually unfolding saga of empowerment and enlightenment. It's a thrilling future, and it beckons to each of us to engage, adapt, and thrive.

Encouraging Lifelong Learning and Adaptability

As we've traversed the expansive landscape of Personal Knowledge Management, a recurring theme has been its adaptability and capacity for evolution. The endgame of PKM is not simply to create a well-organized repository of existing knowledge; rather, it's to establish a vibrant, living system that continues to grow and adapt throughout your lifetime. This goal aligns closely with the larger ethos of lifelong learning and adaptability. It's an orientation toward life that can serve you well in an increasingly complex and fast-paced world. Let's explore how this orientation toward perpetual learning manifests itself.

The Changing Landscape of Learning: Recognizing that Knowledge Isn't Static and Emphasizing the Need for Continuous Adaptation

The days when education was viewed as a finite period confined to early years are long past. In our modern world, knowledge is neither static nor fixed; it's a fluid entity that constantly evolves. Industries change, technologies become obsolete, and the cultural zeitgeist shifts. In such an environment, a 'set it and forget it' approach to learning is untenable. Continuous adaptation is not merely an asset; it's a necessity. Your PKM system serves as an excellent reminder of this reality. The very act of updating your PKM—adding new insights, pruning outdated information, and revisiting your organizing principles—echoes the larger life skill of adaptability. It trains you to be comfortable with change and teaches you the essential art of continuous learning.

Cultivating a Growth Mindset: Embracing Challenges and Viewing Failures as Opportunities for Learning and Growth

One of the underlying principles of lifelong learning is a growth mindset, the belief that abilities and intelligence can be developed through dedication and hard work. This mindset is particularly relevant in the context of PKM. When you encounter a new challenge, whether it's a complex project at work or a personal goal, your first step is likely to consult your PKM system. And when things don't go as planned, it's your PKM that can help you analyze what went wrong and how you can learn from it. Challenges and failures become less about setbacks and more about opportunities for growth. Each difficulty you face becomes a knowledge-building experience, enriching your PKM and, by extension, your understanding of the world.

The Power of Curiosity: Encouraging an Insatiable Appetite for Knowledge and Exploration Throughout Life

If there's one trait that lifelong learners share, it's an insatiable curiosity. It's this desire to explore, to understand, and to delve deeper that fuels the continuous quest for knowledge. Curiosity isn't just about finding answers; it's also about questioning existing assumptions and daring to explore unknown terrains. Your PKM system can serve as a catalyst for this curiosity. Every article you save, every insight you jot down, and every question you note for future exploration is a testament to your curious spirit. This continuous engagement with the world around you enriches not just your PKM but also your life experience.

As we consider the possibilities that a life steeped in continuous learning offers, we realize that PKM is more than a tool; it's a philosophy for intentional living. It encourages us to be adaptable in the face of change, to embrace challenges as avenues for growth, and to nurture an ever-curious mindset that relishes the ongoing journey of discovery. These are not just skills for effective knowledge management; they're skills for a fulfilling, meaningful life. So, as we conclude our exploration of PKM, let this be our lasting takeaway: In a world that never ceases to change, let us pledge never to cease learning, growing, and adapting. For it is in this continual process of becoming that we find our truest selves and our most meaningful successes.

Personal Stories of Transformation through Effective PKM

As a fitting capstone to our exploration of Personal Knowledge Management, let's turn our attention to the lived experiences of individuals who have successfully integrated PKM into their lives, resulting in transformative outcomes. These stories serve as a testament to the practical applications of PKM, illustrating its impact across various walks of life— from the professional to the personal, from the entrepreneurial to the intellectually curious.

The Young Professional: Navigating the Corporate Ladder with a Robust PKM System

Meet Sarah, a young professional in the tech industry. Her entry into the corporate world was fraught with the typical challenges—cutthroat competition, a steep learning curve, and the daunting task of making a mark in a sea of talent. But what set Sarah apart was her meticulously organized PKM system. Over time, she had gathered a wealth of knowledge ranging from industry trends and project management techniques to soft skills like negotiation and conflict resolution. She relied on her PKM to prepare for meetings, lead projects, and even mentor new team members. This structured approach not only helped her excel in her job but also caught the eye of her superiors. Within a couple of years, Sarah was climbing the corporate ladder at an accelerated pace, thanks in no small part to her effective use of PKM.

The Aspiring Entrepreneur: Turning Ideas into Reality by Leveraging Structured Knowledge

Next, we have Raj, who dreamed of starting his own sustainable energy venture. Armed with technical expertise but little business acumen, the path seemed treacherous. But Raj's PKM system became his secret weapon. It was where he stored market research, business strategies, potential pitfalls, and investor profiles. He continuously refined this knowledge, analyzing successful and failed startups and learning from the experiences of industry leaders. When the time came to pitch to investors, his well-structured knowledge paid off. Raj could answer questions confidently, demonstrating not just his passion but also his preparedness.

Today, his startup is a burgeoning success story, proving the power of structured knowledge in turning dreams into reality.

The Lifelong Learner: The Journey of an Individual Who, Irrespective of Profession, Harnessed PKM for Personal Growth and Satisfaction

Laura, a teacher by profession, embodies the spirit of the lifelong learner. For her, PKM is not just about professional development but personal growth. Whether it's literature, philosophy, psychology, or even gardening, her PKM system is a treasure trove of diverse knowledge. This structured approach to learning has enriched her life in countless ways. It has made her a more empathetic educator, a more informed citizen, and above all, a more fulfilled individual. Laura's story serves as a reminder that the ultimate utility of PKM extends beyond our jobs and into the very quality of our lives.

The Digital Nomad: Using PKM to Juggle Diverse Roles, Locations, and Cultures, While Staying Grounded in a Digital Knowledge Base

Finally, there's Alex, a digital nomad who juggles multiple freelance roles while traveling the globe. For him, PKM is more than a tool; it's his anchor in a life characterized by constant change. From client details and project timelines to travel plans and cultural notes, everything is meticulously organized in his digital PKM system. No matter where he is in the world, Alex can access this centralized repository of knowledge, making his nomadic lifestyle not just manageable but truly enriching.

These stories bring to life the transformative potential of Personal Knowledge Management. They prove that PKM is not a mere academic concept but a practical, powerful tool that can bring about tangible change in real-world scenarios. Whether you're a young professional, an aspiring entrepreneur, a lifelong learner, or someone seeking to navigate the complexities of a globalized world, PKM offers something of value. It serves as a scaffold for your ambitions, a map for your explorations, and a compass for your life journey. So, as you turn the final page of this book, consider this not as an end, but as a beginning—the start of your own transformative journey through the empowering world of Personal Knowledge Management.

A Call to Action: Your Personal Knowledge Legacy

As we reach the conclusion of our exploration into Personal Knowledge Management, it's important to look beyond the immediate benefits and practicalities. There's a larger, grander vision at play, one that transforms your individual PKM practice into something akin to a legacy—a lasting imprint of your life's learnings, experiences, and contributions. In this broader frame, each piece of knowledge you acquire, synthesize, and share becomes part of a continuum, a legacy that extends far beyond the boundaries of your own life.

Recognizing that the Knowledge We Acquire, Synthesize, and Share Contributes to Our Personal Legacy

In every domain of human endeavor—be it science, art, politics, or business—the individuals we remember are those who have made a lasting impact. Often, this impact is a direct result of their relationship with knowledge. They were thinkers, innovators, leaders, and, most importantly, learners. Your PKM system serves as a concrete manifestation of your own intellectual journey, a curated exhibit of your lifelong engagement with the world around you. While the knowledge itself may be diverse, the unifying thread is you—the lens through which this knowledge is filtered, synthesized, and applied. As such, your PKM becomes an integral part of your personal legacy, a testament to your intellectual curiosity, your professional achievements, and your broader contributions to society.

The Ripple Effect: Understanding How Our Individual Knowledge Practices Can Influence Communities, Organizations, and Even Industries

Your individual PKM practice does not exist in a vacuum. Each insight you share, each methodology you develop, and even each question you ask can have ripple effects that extend beyond your immediate sphere. Imagine the transformative potential if the best practices you develop become industry standards, or if the mentorship you offer launches the career of the next visionary in your field. Even at the most basic level, the way you organize and apply knowledge can serve as a model for your peers, inspiring them to embark on their own PKM journeys. In this sense, your PKM practice can be a catalyst for broader change, influencing communities, shaping organizations, and even redefining industries.

Inspiring Readers to Embark on Their Unique PKM Journey, Tailoring Practices to Fit Their Goals, Aspirations, and Contexts

As we close this chapter and this book, the ultimate message is one of empowerment and possibility. PKM is not a one-size-fits-all blueprint but a flexible framework that you can tailor to fit your unique circumstances, goals, and aspirations. Whether you're a student, a young professional, an entrepreneur, or someone in the twilight of an illustrious career, the journey is yours to undertake and the legacy yours to build.

So, as you set down this book, consider picking up the mantle of action. Start small if you must—perhaps with a simple digital notebook or a curated reading list—but start. Gradually expand your system to encompass the broad tapestry of your life's interests, challenges, and dreams. Engage with the world as an active knowledge manager, mindful not just of the information you consume but also of the wisdom you generate and share.

May this book serve as the catalyst for your own odyssey into the empowering world of Personal Knowledge Management. It's a journey that promises not just enhanced productivity and professional success, but a richer, more meaningful life. Take that first step today, and in doing so, begin crafting a legacy of knowledge that will serve you and the world in innumerable ways for years to come.

As we reach the concluding lines of this book, the first expression that comes to mind is one of profound gratitude. Thank you for investing your time and intellectual energy into exploring the multifaceted world of Personal Knowledge Management with me. Your engagement with these pages signifies more than just an interest in organizational techniques or productivity hacks; it reveals a deeper commitment to embracing a structured approach to knowledge as a lifelong endeavor.

But even as we close this chapter, let's not forget that the world around us is an ever-unfolding tapestry of knowledge, filled with mysteries to solve, disciplines to explore, and insights to glean. The corpus of human understanding is both vast and endlessly enriching, continually expanding through new discoveries, reinterpretations, and syntheses. This inexhaustible reserve of knowledge offers each of us an open invitation— an invitation to dive deep, to explore with abandon, and to make our unique contributions.

So, may your commitment to Personal Knowledge Management be the key that unlocks doors to uncharted territories of understanding and experience. May it serve as your compass in life's labyrinthine journey, guiding you toward goals you've yet to envision and milestones you've yet to achieve. And as you journey forward, remember that knowledge gains its greatest value when it is shared. In sharing, you enrich not just your own life but also those of others, fostering a community of learning that can uplift us all.

Thank you once again for accompanying me on this enriching journey through the empowering landscape of Personal Knowledge Management. Here's to your continued curiosity, growth, and the countless adventures that surely lie ahead. May you forever be a seeker, a learner, and a sharer, crafting a legacy of wisdom that stands as a beacon for others to follow.

Appendices

Welcome to the appendices, an important addendum designed to complement and enrich the main content of this book. Here, we offer supplementary tools and insights that aim to further illuminate the practical aspects of Personal Knowledge Management. Whether it's templates for organizing your information, recommended software for efficient knowledge storage, or detailed case studies offering real-world applications of PKM principles, this section seeks to provide you with tangible resources for immediate use.

The purpose of including these appendices is not to overwhelm you with additional information but to offer a ready-to-use toolkit that can make your initiation into PKM a smoother, more intuitive process. Consider these resources as foundational aids that you can refer back to, adapt, and build upon as you make progress on your PKM journey.

The journey toward effective Personal Knowledge Management is rarely a solitary endeavor, and it often benefits from a variety of tools and perspectives. It's my hope that these supplementary materials will serve as valuable allies in your ongoing quest for knowledge mastery. Feel free to delve into them as you see fit, either in a sequential manner or by cherry-picking those resources most pertinent to your current needs and queries.

So, as you prepare to close this book and open the doors to your unique PKM adventure, let these appendices be your guideposts, offering you both direction and inspiration. Use them to lay a strong foundation, to troubleshoot challenges, and to deepen your understanding of this transformative practice. Here's to enriching your PKM journey with these additional layers of insight and practicality.

Recommended Reading and Resources on PKM

One of the most empowering aspects of Personal Knowledge Management is that it is a discipline continually enriched by new perspectives, tools, and methodologies. Whether you're a newcomer to PKM or an experienced practitioner looking to deepen your understanding, the following recommended reading and resources offer a wealth of valuable insights to augment your journey.

Books: A Curated List of Seminal and Contemporary Works

Books offer an in-depth exploration of themes and ideas, and there are several seminal and contemporary works that can deepen your understanding of PKM, knowledge management, and learning methodologies. From foundational texts that lay out the principles of knowledge management to modern takes that incorporate technology and societal shifts, these books serve as valuable companions for anyone serious about mastering PKM.

Foundational Books:"How to Take Smart Notes" by Sönke Ahrens

A foundational text for understanding the Zettelkasten method, a specific approach to PKM, and learning how to effectively take notes and manage knowledge.

"Personal Knowledge Management: Individual, Organizational and Social Perspectives" by David J. Pauleen and Gary E. Gorman

An academic perspective on PKM with insights on its various dimensions, such as individual, organizational, and social aspects.

"Getting Things Done: The Art of Stress-Free Productivity" by David Allen

While primarily a book on productivity, GTD includes crucial concepts applicable to PKM such as organizing tasks, information, and incoming items.

Books on Related Concepts:

"The Organized Mind: Thinking Straight in the Age of Information Overload" by Daniel J. Levitin

This book offers insights into organizing information, thoughts, and tasks effectively, which is crucial for efficient Personal Knowledge Management.

"Deep Work: Rules for Focused Success in a Distracted World" by Cal Newport

This book delves into methods and practices to improve focus and manage knowledge effectively in the midst of distractions.

"Make It Stick: The Science of Successful Learning" by Peter C. Brown, Henry L. Roediger III, and Mark A. McDaniel

This book explores strategies and methodologies for effective learning, a key component of personal knowledge management.

Articles: Highlighting Insightful Contributions

The field of PKM is regularly enriched by thought-provoking articles penned by thought leaders, researchers, and practitioners. These pieces often present cutting-edge ideas, analyze emerging trends, or offer fresh perspectives on established theories. Whether published in academic journals, industry magazines, or online platforms, such articles serve as shorter yet impactful reads that can broaden your understanding of specific PKM topics.

General Overviews and Strategies

"The Importance of Personal Knowledge Management in the Knowledge Society"

Offers a general overview of PKM concepts and its importance in today's knowledge-intensive society.

"PKM: A Learning Theory for the Knowledge Society"

Explores the conceptual underpinnings of PKM as a learning theory and how it prepares individuals for the knowledge society.

"Personal Knowledge Management: A Research Agenda" by Wright

Summary: This article explores the need for a greater focus on the individual in knowledge management research, postulating that personal knowledge management (PKM) can serve as a conceptual framework for understanding how individuals manage information and knowledge. It provides a comprehensive overview of PKM, its importance, and suggests areas where further research is needed.

"The Role of Technology in Personal Knowledge Management" by Dr. Tony Wilson

Summary: This piece delves into how technology can support PKM by allowing for more efficient storage, organization, retrieval, and sharing of knowledge. It addresses the selection of appropriate tools and technologies based on individual needs and preferences and discusses the importance of being mindful of the limitations and potential pitfalls of technology in managing personal knowledge.

"Personal Knowledge Management: The Foundation of Organizational Knowledge Management" by Pauleen and Gorman

Summary: The authors argue that effective organizational knowledge management is rooted in strong personal knowledge management practices. They offer insights into how PKM can empower employees and improve organizational knowledge sharing and utilization, emphasizing the need for organizations to support and encourage PKM practices among their staff.

"Principles of Effective Personal Knowledge Management" by Smith

Summary: This article discusses fundamental principles that underpin effective PKM, focusing on strategies like efficient information acquisition, storage, application, and sharing. It provides practical tips and advice on how individuals can implement these principles to optimize their personal knowledge management efforts.

"PKM in the Age of Digital Learning" by Siadaty, Jovanović, and Pata

Summary: The article explores the role and implications of PKM in today's digital learning environments. It examines how PKM practices can support lifelong learning and help individuals adapt to the rapidly changing knowledge landscape, discussing the integration of PKM with formal and informal learning experiences.

"Building a Smarter To-Do List, Part I" by Merlin Mann

Summary: This article, part of a series, provides insights and tips on creating more effective to-do lists as a part of personal knowledge management. It touches on prioritization, context, and efficiency, providing a practical guide to managing tasks and information better.

"Mind Mapping as a Tool in Personal Knowledge Management" by Maryam Tayebinik and Marlia Puteh

Summary: The authors investigate mind mapping as a powerful tool for PKM, discussing its utility in organizing, representing, and recalling information. The article provides an overview of mind mapping principles and techniques and explores their application in managing personal knowledge more effectively.

Websites and Blogs for Additional Articles:

Medium: Offers numerous articles on PKM from various authors, focusing on different aspects and approaches.

Harold Jarche's Blog: Harold Jarche is a recognized expert in the field of knowledge management, and his blog features numerous articles and insights on PKM.

Lifehacker: This site often has articles related to productivity and knowledge management, offering practical tips and advice.

Online Courses: Comprehensive Learning Opportunities

If you prefer a more structured approach to learning, there are numerous online courses available that offer comprehensive lessons on various facets of PKM. These courses range from introductory modules that cover the basics of information organization to advanced classes that delve into complex PKM strategies and tools. Whether you're looking for free resources to get started or are willing to invest in more specialized courses, you'll find options to fit your needs and aspirations.

Coursera

Course Title: Learning How to Learn: Powerful mental tools to help you master tough subjects

Summary: While not directly labeled as a PKM course, this very popular course teaches principles that are foundational to effective PKM, including memory techniques, dealing with procrastination, and optimizing learning.

Instructor: Dr. Barbara Oakley and Dr. Terrence Sejnowski

Udemy

Course Title: Personal Knowledge Management (PKM)

Summary: This course typically covers the basics of PKM, including techniques for managing personal information and knowledge, organization methods, and practical applications of PKM concepts.

Instructor: Various, depending on the current availability of courses on the platform.

LinkedIn Learning

Course Title: Personal Effectiveness Tips

Summary: It provides insights and tips on time management, organization, and productivity, which are critical components of effective PKM.

Instructor: Dave Crenshaw

Skillshare

Skillshare often has courses related to productivity, learning, and knowledge management, which can help in building and refining your PKM system. Specific course titles and instructors can vary, so browse the platform for the most current offerings.

YouTube & Other Free Online Resources

You might find free tutorials and lectures on PKM by experts and practitioners in the field. Searching for terms like "Personal Knowledge Management," "Effective Learning Techniques," or "Information Management" can yield helpful results.

Tiago Forte's Building a Second Brain

Course Title: Building a Second Brain

Summary: Tiago Forte's course is renowned in the productivity and PKM communities. It provides extensive insights into managing information overload, organizing digital notes, and creating a "second brain" to augment your natural cognitive abilities.

When choosing a course, consider your learning goals, preferred learning style, and the time you can dedicate to learning. Some courses might be more theory-oriented, while others might focus more on practical applications and offer hands-on exercises. Keep abreast of new courses and updates as the field of PKM is continually evolving with advancements in technology and our understanding of learning and cognition.

Podcasts: Engage with the Auditory Dimension of PKM

Podcasts offer a unique auditory experience for absorbing information and are increasingly becoming a popular medium for intellectual enrichment. Relevant podcasts on PKM often feature interviews with experts, thought leaders, and innovators in the field. These discussions can offer you a behind-the-scenes look at the real-world applications of PKM, as well as practical tips, strategies, and even some inspirational stories to motivate your own PKM journey.

Podcasts and Webinars:

Various podcasts and webinars discuss topics related to PKM. Listening to interviews with experts and discussions on PKM concepts and strategies can complement your learning from formal courses.

Websites and Blogs: Stay Updated with the Latest

For those who prefer up-to-the-minute information, dedicated websites and blogs focused on PKM offer a wealth of regularly updated content. From reviews of the latest PKM tools to articles on emerging trends and techniques, these platforms are treasure troves of information for anyone keen to keep their finger on the pulse of the PKM world.

By utilizing a mix of these resources, you can cultivate a well-rounded, multi-dimensional understanding of Personal Knowledge Management. As you continue on your PKM journey, these books, articles, courses, podcasts, and digital platforms can serve as your constant companions, offering both foundational knowledge and cutting-edge insights. Feel free to explore these resources at your own pace and in accordance with your own interests, and may they enrich your quest for knowledge mastery.

Blogs and Websites:

Blogs like Forte Labs and websites of PKM practitioners often host a wealth of information, tutorials, and insights on PKM, which can serve as informal, self-paced learning resources.

Forums and Communities:

Participating in forums like Reddit's Personal Knowledge Management can offer community support, diverse perspectives, and resources for learning about PKM.

Glossary of PKM Terms and Tools

Understanding the terminology associated with Personal Knowledge Management is a crucial first step in mastering the practice. Additionally, getting familiar with the various tools available can aid you in developing an effective PKM system tailored to your needs. Below is a glossary of key terms and tools commonly used in the field of PKM.

Terms:

Aggregation:

Aggregation refers to the process of collecting or gathering disparate pieces of information from various sources into one centralized location. In PKM, this could mean pulling together articles, research papers, podcast episodes, or social media threads that are relevant to a particular topic or project you're working on.

Curation:

Curation involves selecting, organizing, and presenting information for a specific purpose. Unlike aggregation, which is simply gathering data, curation adds a layer of editorial judgment. In the context of PKM, curation could mean sifting through your aggregated data to extract what's most relevant, meaningful, or insightful and arranging it in a way that's easy for you to access and apply later.

Tools:

Notion:

Notion is a versatile tool that serves as an all-in-one workspace for note-taking, task management, databases, and more. It offers a range of features such as nested pages, tagging, and rich media support, making it highly customizable for PKM. With Notion, you can create a centralized space for all your knowledge assets, making it easier to manage and retrieve information.

Roam Research:

Roam Research is a note-taking tool designed with networked thought in mind. It allows for easy linking between notes, creating a web-like structure of interconnected ideas. Roam Research is highly applicable in PKM for its capabilities to surface relationships between different pieces of information, which can be especially useful for synthesis and application of knowledge.

Templates and Checklists for Setting Up a PKM System

As you embark on your PKM journey, the following templates and checklists can offer a structured approach, ensuring that you don't overlook any critical steps and that you maintain a consistent routine for managing your knowledge.

Initial Setup Checklist:

This step-by-step list guides you through the essential stages of setting up your PKM system, from selecting a tool and defining your knowledge domains to creating an organization structure and setting reminders for regular updates.

Setting up a Personal Knowledge Management (PKM) system involves several considerations, including selecting the right tools, determining the processes, and categorizing the information effectively.

Below is a checklist to help you with the initial setup:

1. Define Objectives and Goals

- Determine the primary purpose of your PKM system.
- List the specific goals you want to achieve with your PKM system.

2. Select Suitable Tools

- Choose a note-taking tool (e.g., Evernote, Notion, OneNote).
- Decide on a reading and research tool (e.g., Pocket, Instapaper).
- Opt for a task management tool (e.g., Todoist, Trello).
- Choose storage and backup solutions (e.g., Google Drive, Dropbox).

3. Establish Processes

- Develop a routine for daily learning and knowledge acquisition.
- Create a process for taking notes and synthesizing information.
- Define a method for reviewing and revising your notes regularly.
- Establish a workflow for archiving, deleting, or updating outdated or irrelevant information.

4. Organize Information Effectively

- Decide on a categorization or tagging system.
- Create templates for different types of notes (e.g., book summaries, article reviews).
- Set up folders, notebooks, or databases for different knowledge areas or subjects.
- Develop an indexing system for easy retrieval of information.

5. Set Up a Reflection and Review Routine

- Allocate specific times for reflection on newly acquired knowledge.
- Establish a schedule for regular review and revision of your notes.
- Create a process for synthesizing and integrating new knowledge with existing knowledge.
- Decide on a method for tracking your learning progress and goals.

6. Develop a Knowledge Sharing Mechanism

- Choose platforms or mediums for sharing your knowledge (e.g., blog, social media).
- Define the audience for your shared knowledge.
- Develop a schedule for regular knowledge sharing.
- Create guidelines or criteria for what to share and how to share.

7. Create Backup and Security Measures

- Set up regular backups for your PKM system.
- Choose secure passwords and enable two-factor authentication where available.
- Regularly update software and applications to the latest versions.
- Develop a recovery plan in case of data loss or system failure.

8. Plan for Continuous Improvement

- Set milestones for evaluating the effectiveness of your PKM system.
- Regularly seek feedback from peers or mentors on your PKM practices.
- Continuously look for new tools, methods, or strategies to enhance your PKM system.
- Adjust and refine your PKM system based on learning needs, goals, and preferences.

9. Documentation

- Document your PKM processes, workflows, and systems clearly.

- Regularly update your documentation to reflect any changes or adjustments.
- Make your documentation easily accessible within your PKM system.

10. Testing and Iteration

- Test your PKM system to ensure all components work seamlessly together.
- Regularly review your PKM setup to identify areas for improvement or optimization.
- Iterate on your system based on feedback, new insights, or changing needs.

Remember, the above checklist is a starting point. You might need to customize it based on your unique needs, learning style, and preferences. The key is to keep iterating and optimizing your system as you go along and as you become more clear on what works best for you.

Daily/Weekly PKM Routine Template:

To keep your PKM system vibrant and useful, consistency is key. This template offers suggested routines for daily and weekly knowledge management activities, such as capturing new information, reviewing saved content, and reflecting on what you've learned. The template is customizable, allowing you to align it with your personal preferences and life rhythms.

Creating a daily/weekly PKM routine involves allocating time for learning, processing information, organizing knowledge, and reflecting on it. Below is a template that you can customize according to your preferences, priorities, and schedule. This is just a starting point; feel free to modify it as per your needs.

Daily Routine:

Morning:

1. Review Goals and Priorities

   - Quickly review your long-term goals and the priorities for the day.
   - Allocate time blocks for learning and knowledge management activities.

2. Learning Session (30 mins to 1 hr)

   - Read articles, books, or watch educational videos.
   - Take structured notes during or immediately after learning.

3. Process Inbox (15-30 mins)

   - Go through your PKM "inbox" where you collect ideas, notes, articles, etc.
   - Organize and categorize new information.
   - Delete irrelevant or unneeded items.

Afternoon:

1. Quick Review (15 mins)

   - Review the information processed in the morning.
   - Adjust tasks and priorities if needed.

2. Learning Session (30 mins to 1 hr)

   - Continue with learning activities, focusing on different subjects or sources.
   - Summarize or reflect on the knowledge acquired.

3. Organize & Synthesize (30 mins)

   - Organize the information learned and integrate it with existing knowledge.
   - Create connections, mind maps, or synthesize insights.

Evening:

1. Reflect & Plan (15-30 mins)
   - Reflect on what you have learned and how it can be applied.
   - Plan the next day's learning and PKM activities.
   - Update your goals and task list based on new insights.

Weekly Routine:

Weekend or a Chosen Day:

1. Review & Reflect (1-2 hrs)

   - Review the knowledge acquired throughout the week.
   - Reflect on its relevance and applications.
   - Identify gaps in understanding or areas for further exploration.
2. Organize & Synthesize (1-2 hrs)

   - Organize accumulated information.
   - Synthesize knowledge across different sources and create connections.
   - Update your knowledge base, mind maps, or other organizational tools.
3. Plan & Set Goals (30 mins to 1 hr)

   - Plan learning and PKM activities for the next week.
   - Set goals and priorities based on current needs and long-term objectives.
   - Allocate time blocks for focused learning and knowledge management activities.
4. Maintenance & Cleanup (30 mins to 1 hr)

   - Clean up your PKM system.
   - Archive or delete outdated or irrelevant information.
   - Update and optimize organizational structures, tags, categories, etc.

Tips:

- Flexibility: Adjust time blocks and activities based on your energy levels, schedule, and priorities.
- Consistency: Regular, even if small, daily and weekly activities are more effective than irregular, intensive sessions.
- Integration: Integrate PKM activities with your work, studies, or other commitments.
- Tool Selection: Choose tools and platforms that support your PKM routine and adapt them as your needs evolve.
- Iteration: Regularly review and update your routine to accommodate changes in your goals, preferences, and lifestyle.

Knowledge Audit Template:

Regularly assessing your current knowledge base can help you identify gaps and set future learning goals. This template provides a structured format to make this audit process systematic and actionable.

A Knowledge Audit is a systematic examination and evaluation of organizational or personal knowledge needs, existing knowledge assets or resources, future knowledge needs, and the flows of knowledge. It helps in identifying any gaps, redundancies, and opportunities for improvement. Below is a basic template for a Personal Knowledge Audit that you can customize according to your needs.

Personal Knowledge Audit Template:

I. Personal Details

1. Name:
2. Date:
3. Objective/Purpose of the Audit:

II. Knowledge Needs Assessment

1. Learning Goals & Objectives:

- What knowledge or skills am I aiming to acquire or develop?
- Why are these important for my personal or professional development?

2. Areas of Interest:

- What subjects or fields am I interested in?
- What topics do I want to explore further?

3. Knowledge Gaps:

- What are the areas where I lack sufficient knowledge or understanding?
- What skills do I need to develop or improve?

III. Existing Knowledge Inventory

1. Knowledge Assets:

- What are my existing knowledge, skills, and competencies?
- What information, resources, or tools do I currently have access to?

2. Knowledge Organization:

- How is my existing knowledge organized and managed?
- What tools or systems do I use for Personal Knowledge Management (PKM)?

3. Knowledge Accessibility:

- How easily can I access and retrieve my existing knowledge assets?
- Are there any barriers or challenges in accessing my knowledge?

IV. Knowledge Acquisition & Learning Methods

1. Learning Preferences:

- What are my preferred learning styles and methods?

- What learning environments are most conducive to my knowledge acquisition?

2. Learning Resources & Tools:

- What resources, tools, or platforms do I use for learning?
- What additional resources or tools do I need to acquire knowledge effectively?

3. Learning Plan:

- How do I plan my learning activities?
- What strategies do I use to acquire and retain knowledge?

V. Knowledge Sharing & Application

1. Knowledge Sharing:

- How do I share my knowledge with others?
- What platforms or mediums do I use for knowledge dissemination?

2. Knowledge Application:

- How do I apply my acquired knowledge in real-life situations or work?
- What are the challenges in applying my knowledge effectively?

VI. Action Plan

1. Knowledge Development Goals:

- Define specific goals and objectives for knowledge development.
- Identify priority areas for learning and development.

2. Strategies & Actions:

- Outline specific strategies and actions to achieve knowledge development goals.
- Identify resources, tools, and support needed to implement the action plan.

3. Timeline & Milestones:

    - Define a timeline for implementing the action plan.
    - Set milestones for monitoring progress and achieving learning goals.

VII. Review & Update

1. Review Date(s):

    - When will I review my progress against the action plan?
    - How frequently will I update my knowledge audit?

2. Update Mechanism:

    - How will I update my knowledge audit based on new learnings, changes in goals, or shifts in priorities?
    - What mechanisms will I use to ensure my knowledge audit remains relevant and up-to-date?

VIII. Notes & Reflections

- Any additional notes, reflections, or observations related to the knowledge audit.
- Insights gained during the audit process.

Final Remarks:

- This template is customizable; adapt it to suit your personal context, goals, and preferences.
- Regularly revisiting and updating your knowledge audit is crucial for ensuring it remains relevant and effective in guiding your learning and knowledge management efforts.

Content Curation Template:

Effective curation is an essential aspect of PKM, and this template offers a framework for gathering, filtering, and storing valuable information from a multitude of sources. It will help you decide what to keep, what to discard, and how to organize the kept information for easy retrieval and application.

Content curation involves collecting, organizing, and displaying information relevant to a particular topic or area of interest. Here is a simple template to help you curate content effectively. This template can be adapted to suit various platforms such as a blog, newsletter, or a personal knowledge management system.

Content Curation Template:

1. Content Information

Title:

- Title of the content.

Author/Creator:

- Name of the content creator or author.

Source/Platform:

- Where the content was published or shared.

Publication Date:

- When the content was originally published.

Link/URL:

- Direct link to the original content.

2. Summary & Key Points

Brief Summary:

- A concise summary of the content, capturing the main ideas, arguments, or findings.

Key Points:

- Bullet list of the most important points, insights, or takeaways from the content.

3. Relevance & Application

Relevance:

- Why is this content relevant to your audience or to your personal learning goals?
- How does it relate to other content you have curated or your broader area of interest?

Application:

- How can the knowledge or insights from this content be applied in real-life situations or professional contexts?
- Any practical tips, strategies, or advice offered in the content.

4. Reflection & Analysis

Personal Reflection:

- Your thoughts, opinions, or interpretations of the content.
- Any agreements, disagreements, or further insights you have.

Analysis:

- A critical analysis of the content's arguments, methodologies, or conclusions.
- Any limitations, biases, or areas for further exploration identified in the content.

5. Category & Tags

Category:

- The main subject or theme of the content (e.g., Productivity, Technology, Health).

Tags/Keywords:

- Specific tags or keywords associated with the content (e.g., Time Management, Artificial Intelligence, Mental Wellness).

6. Visuals & Additional Resources

Visuals:

- Any images, charts, graphs, or videos included in the content.
- Visual summary or infographic if available.

Additional Resources:

- Links to related articles, studies, or resources mentioned in the content.
- Any supplementary materials, references, or readings recommended by the author/creator.

7. Action Items & Next Steps

Action Items:

- Specific actions you plan to take based on the insights from the content.
- Any follow-up tasks, readings, or research prompted by the content.

Next Steps:

- Plans for sharing, discussing, or further exploring the content.
- Any additional content curation or creation inspired by the content.

Final Notes:

- Adjust the template sections according to the type of content you are curating and the platform you are using.
- Remember to give proper attribution to the original creators or authors and to respect intellectual property rights when curating content.
- Regularly review and update your curated content to ensure its relevance and accuracy over time.

Reflection and Synthesis Template:

Absorbing information is just the first step in knowledge management. To truly make it your own, reflection and synthesis are crucial. This template provides guided prompts to help you process new information, integrate it into your existing knowledge framework, and consider its applications or implications.

A Reflection and Synthesis template can be instrumental in consolidating learning and making connections between different pieces of knowledge. It can aid in creating a coherent understanding and application of learned concepts. Here's a simple template that can help you in reflective synthesis:

Reflection and Synthesis Template:

1. Content Information

Title/Topic:

- Title or the main topic of the content or subject you're reflecting on.

Source(s)/Reference(s):

- Citations or links to the original source(s) of information or content.

Date:

- The date of reflection and synthesis.

2. Summary of Learning

Key Concepts:

- A concise summary of the main ideas, principles, or concepts learned.

Details and Nuances:

- A brief outline of the specific details, nuances, or subtleties of the learned content.

3. Synthesis

Connections:

- How does this new learning connect to what I already know?
- Are there conflicting ideas or concepts between the new and previous learning?

Integration:

- How can I integrate this new knowledge with my existing knowledge base?
- Are there common themes or patterns emerging from different pieces of learned content?

Implications:

- What are the broader implications of this new knowledge?
- How does it impact my understanding of related subjects or fields?

4. Critical Reflection

Insights:

- What new insights or perspectives have emerged from this learning?
- How has it challenged or reinforced my existing beliefs or assumptions?

Questions and Curiosities:

- What questions or curiosities have arisen from this learning?
- What areas do I want to explore further or understand more deeply?

5. Application and Implementation

Practical Applications:

- How can I apply this new knowledge in real-world situations or professional contexts?
- What practical strategies or techniques can be derived from this learning?

Action Steps:

- What specific actions will I take to implement this new knowledge?
- How will I integrate this learning into my daily routines or practices?

6. Review and Revision

Reflection on Reflection:

- How effective was this reflection and synthesis process?
- What could I have done differently to enhance my understanding?

Plan for Revision:

- How will I revisit and revise this reflection and synthesis?
- What schedule or triggers will remind me to review and update my understanding?

7. Final Thoughts/Additional Notes

- Any other thoughts, comments, or notes related to the learning, reflection, and synthesis process.

Conclusion:

- This template is a guide and should be modified based on personal preferences, specific needs, or particular contexts.
- Regular reflection and synthesis are crucial for deepening understanding, making connections between disparate pieces of knowledge, and enhancing learning retention and application.
- Integrating this process into your learning routine can significantly augment your Personal Knowledge Management practices.

These templates and checklists are not meant to be rigid rules but rather starting points that you can customize to suit your unique PKM needs and preferences. Feel free to adapt them as you see fit and as you grow more comfortable and experienced in your PKM practices.

As we wrap up these appendices and bring our comprehensive exploration of Personal Knowledge Management to a close, remember that the resources provided here are not a one-off read. They're designed to serve as an evolving toolkit, intended to be revisited, consulted, and adapted as you mature in your PKM journey. Whether you're just starting out or are looking to refine an already robust system, these supplementary materials can offer valuable insights and practical aid.

While these appendices give you a solid foundation, always keep in mind that the true power of PKM is in its personalisation. It's in the tweaks, adjustments, and customization's that you introduce to make the system resonate with your unique context, aspirations, and challenges. Personal Knowledge Management, at its core, is a deeply individual endeavor.

So, as you turn the page to embark on or continue your unique journey, let these appendices serve as both a guide and a companion. May they assist you in laying down a solid foundation, and may they inspire you to build a PKM practice that's as individual and transformative as you are. Thank you for allowing this book to be a part of your journey toward knowledge mastery and personal growth.

Checklist to help you with the initial setup:

1. Define Objectives and Goals

- Determine the primary purpose of your PKM system.
- List the specific goals you want to achieve with your PKM system.

2. Select Suitable Tools

- Choose a note-taking tool (e.g., Evernote, Notion, OneNote).
- Decide on a reading and research tool (e.g., Pocket, Instapaper).
- Opt for a task management tool (e.g., Todoist, Trello).
- Choose storage and backup solutions (e.g., Google Drive, Dropbox).

3. Establish Processes

- Develop a routine for daily learning and knowledge acquisition.
- Create a process for taking notes and synthesizing information.
- Define a method for reviewing and revising your notes regularly.
- Establish a workflow for archiving, deleting, or updating outdated or irrelevant information.

4. Organize Information Effectively

- Decide on a categorization or tagging system.
- Create templates for different types of notes (e.g., book summaries, article reviews).
- Set up folders, notebooks, or databases for different knowledge areas or subjects.
- Develop an indexing system for easy retrieval of information.

5. Set Up a Reflection and Review Routine

- Allocate specific times for reflection on newly acquired knowledge.
- Establish a schedule for regular review and revision of your notes.
- Create a process for synthesizing and integrating new knowledge with existing knowledge.
- Decide on a method for tracking your learning progress and goals.

6. Develop a Knowledge Sharing Mechanism

- Choose platforms or mediums for sharing your knowledge (e.g., blog, social media).
- Define the audience for your shared knowledge.
- Develop a schedule for regular knowledge sharing.
- Create guidelines or criteria for what to share and how to share.

7. Create Backup and Security Measures

- Set up regular backups for your PKM system.
- Choose secure passwords and enable two-factor authentication where available.
- Regularly update software and applications to the latest versions.
- Develop a recovery plan in case of data loss or system failure.

8. Plan for Continuous Improvement

- Set milestones for evaluating the effectiveness of your PKM system.
- Regularly seek feedback from peers or mentors on your PKM practices.
- Continuously look for new tools, methods, or strategies to enhance your PKM system.
- Adjust and refine your PKM system based on learning needs, goals, and preferences.

9. Documentation

- Document your PKM processes, workflows, and systems clearly.
- Regularly update your documentation to reflect any changes or adjustments.
- Make your documentation easily accessible within your PKM system.

10. Testing and Iteration

- Test your PKM system to ensure all components work seamlessly together.
- Regularly review your PKM setup to identify areas for improvement or optimization.
- Iterate on your system based on feedback, new insights, or changing needs.

Daily Routine:

Morning:

Review Goals and Priorities

- Quickly review your long-term goals and the priorities for the day.
- Allocate time blocks for learning and knowledge management activities.

Learning Session (30 mins to 1 hr)

- Read articles, books, or watch educational videos.
- Take structured notes during or immediately after learning.

Process Inbox (15-30 mins)

- Go through your PKM "inbox" where you collect ideas, notes, articles, etc.
- Organize and categorize new information.
- Delete irrelevant or unneeded items.

Afternoon:

Quick Review (15 mins)

- Review the information processed in the morning.
- Adjust tasks and priorities if needed

Learning Session (30 mins to 1 hr)

- Continue with learning activities, focusing on different subjects or sources.
- Summarize or reflect on the knowledge acquired.

Organize & Synthesize (30 mins)

- Organize the information learned and integrate it with existing knowledge.
- Create connections, mind maps, or synthesize insights.

Evening:

Reflect & Plan (15-30 mins)

- Reflect on what you have learned and how it can be applied.
- Plan the next day's learning and PKM activities.
- Update your goals and task list based on new insights.

Other Books by T.D. Errol

The Evolving Self: Mastering Continuous Improvement in the Prime of Life

The Power of Checklists: Mastering momentum for Business Success

Decisive Choices: Mastering Strategies for Effective Decision Making and Problem Solving

Digitize Your Life: Embrace Sustainability and Efficiency

Embracing Change and Adapting: The Importance of being open to change and how to adapt to new situations or environments as part of personal growth.

Mastering Communication: A Guide to Developing Effective Communication Skills.

Building Emotional Intelligence: Enhancing Personal and Professional Relationships

Share Your Thoughts with Us!

Dear Reader,

I hope you enjoyed journeying through the pages of my book. Your insights and experiences mean the world to me. If the story resonated with you or if there's any area you feel could be improved, I'd be truly grateful to hear your thoughts.

Please consider leaving a review on Amazon or the platform where you made the purchase. Your feedback not only helps me grow as an author but also guides fellow readers in their choices.

Alternatively, feel free to drop me a personal note at errolpublishing@gmail.com Every word you share contributes to the story's evolving journey.

Thank you for being a cherished part of this adventure.

Warm regards,

T.D. Errol

Author Bio

T.D. Errol is a seasoned author, business strategist, and thought leader based in the stunning landscapes of Colorado. Drawing upon a rich tapestry of experiences from serving as a United States Marine Corps infantryman to holding leadership and managerial roles, T.D. commands a broad spectrum of expertise in business, strategy, and personal development.

Having encountered physical adversities including a major back surgery, T.D. discovered the transformative power of intentional walking as a tool for introspection and recovery. This personal experience birthed a unique theory on walking, which emphasizes the quality and mindfulness of each step over sheer speed or distance.

His profound insights on personal growth and business acumen are deeply rooted in years of on-ground experience, a dedication to continuous learning, and a commitment to staying updated with the latest trends in leadership and management. With a flair for storytelling, T.D. masterfully weaves together lessons from his military background, managerial roles, and personal journeys to provide invaluable wisdom to aspiring leaders and professionals.

Passionate about inspiring others, T.D. Errol combines his vast business knowledge with a genuine desire to uplift and empower. He invites readers and fellow professionals to dive deep into the realms of strategic thinking, leadership, and the boundless potential of personal and professional growth.

Errol Publishing

www.ingramcontent.com/pod-product-compliance
Lightning Source LLC
Chambersburg PA
CBHW072153290526
45794CB00004B/1504